Praise

"Coach Paula's book is a great gift to women of all ages. I have lived all these years and never understood how a man loves, and what a man needs in order to commit. Most valuable is Paula's Cognitive Commitment Component of Men. What a revelation!"

Tricia R, Cleveland Heights, Ohio

"Wow, has Coach Paula opened my eyes! I've wondered about why men relate the way they do all these years. I now feel I have the inside scoop on how to bring out the best in a man. *Why Won't He Commit* is a gem of book that explains how to create a happy, committed relationship – one of the true joys in life."

Deborah M, Missoula, MT

"This book should be required reading for every woman in a relationship. I've read nearly every relationship book out there and this book was an eye-opener for me."

Cheri C., New York, NY

"Having read *The Rules,* I found this book so interesting for mid-term relationships and the pitfalls when men seem to be doing everything right, bar stepping up and committing. An excellent addition to my collection!"

Stephanie C., Suffolk, England

"I've been married for 25 years and bought the book for my daughter but then read it myself. It's such useful information. The Consumer vs Buyer Relationship concept is simply brilliant. It would have saved me from wasting time and energy with the wrong guys before I found my Buyer! I highly recommend this book to women of all ages. It should be required reading for any woman who wants to be in a committed relationship!"

Barbara D., Phoenix, AZ

"This book is a must for any woman who strives to understand the male mind. After reading about the Puppy Principle and the Consumer vs. Buyer Relationship, you'll not only get a glimpse into a man's thought process, but also determine whether he is ready to commit or just having a good time. I will approach dating from a whole new place now!"

Betsy P., Baltimore, MD

"If you've ever wondered why he won't commit and his actions don't align with yours, after reading Paula Grooms book, you'll wonder no more! It takes the guesswork out of why he may love you, but may never take your relationship to the next level. *Why He Won't Commit?* is the intelligent woman's guide to dating smarter with self-esteem all the way to the alter!"

Kathy B., Cornelius, NC

"Why Won't He Commit? presents a wholly unique and accessible approach to understanding the differences between the way men and women approach commitment. I think everyone who reads it will be grateful for the valuable guidance in this book and will be left wanting more from Coach Paula!"

Lori K., New York, NY

"I wish I would have had this book years ago! I could have saved myself a lot of time and tears. I feel like I finally have useful information about men that actually makes sense."

Christine M., Ft. Worth, TX

"I love this book! Thank you to Coach Paula for her amazing insight. As a woman in my thirties, who's dated dozens of men without a clue as to what I was doing, I finally understand and have changed my thinking and approach to men and dating. And it's working!!"

Erin G., Minneapolis, MN

"Life changing information! I'm 47 years old and wish that I had this book at an earlier age, as I could have saved myself from many years of unnecessary headaches and broken relationships. Every young woman should read this book straight out of high school. It can save them decades of trying to figure out this whole relationship thing, which baffles most of us. I'm confident *Why Won't He Commit?* will help millions of women to make better choices in relationships."

Michelle S., Pemberton, NJ

"This is an invaluable book that teaches you to identify what you want in love and get it!"

Brynnleigh F., Boston, MA

WHY
Won't He
COMMIT?

How a Man Decides to Make You "THE ONE"

Coach Paula Grooms

NEW YORK

LONDON • NASHVILLE • MELBOURNE • VANCOUVER

Why Won't He Commit?

Published in New York, New York, by Morgan James Publishing in partnership with Difference Press.
www.MorganJamesPublishing.com

The Morgan James Speakers Group can bring authors to your live event. For more information or to book an event visit The Morgan James Speakers Group at www.TheMorganJamesSpeakersGroup.com.

ISBN 978-1-68350-801-4 paperback
ISBN 978-1-68350-802-1 eBook
Library of Congress Control Number: 2017915898

Cover Design by:
Rachel Lopez

Cover Concept by:
Jennifer Stimson

Interior Design by:
Megan Whitney Dillon
Creative Ninja Designs

In an effort to support local communities, raise awareness and funds, Morgan James.
Publishing donates a percentage of all book sales for the life of each book to
Habitat for Humanity Peninsula and Greater Williamsburg.

Get involved today! Visit
www.MorganJamesBuilds.com

To Milad, a man without whom this book
could not have been written and this woman's heart
could not have been saved.

content

Foreword

When we wrote *The Rules,* we had one simple goal: spread the truth about what it really takes for women to get married. When the book first came out, there were lots of questions. Do The Rules really work? Do I really have to follow <u>all</u> The Rules? Do men really respond differently to women who use The Rules?

Since writing our first book and having it distributed in twenty-seven countries, we have written four more and talked with thousands of women from all over the world. What we've learned confirms why we wrote the first book: The Rules work for women who want to be cherished by men and in committed relationships. We have story after story of happily ever after, thanks to women following The Rules.

We know that the truth can be difficult to hear and even more difficult to follow. We also know that The Rules are not natural for many women and that women who want to get married have a bit of a harder road these days – especially as our society becomes more and more open and women are "expected" to do so many things that are against The Rules. It is why we have trained coaches like Coach Paula Grooms to help women use The Rules. Coach Paula has seen the power of The Rules and helps women apply them to their dating and in their relationships.

Most women are confused and frustrated by men's actions and behaviors. Coach Paula understands how men love, commit, and bond with women and uses her Puppy Principle to explain it from an easily relatable experience most women have had themselves. Coach Paula explains under what circumstances men are ready, willing, and able to commit – or not. Her Consumer vs. Buyer Relationship Theory will help you recognize men who will not commit – despite loving you.

We are most often asked, "Why do The Rules work?" The answer is simply that they do, but if knowing why they do is important to you, we suggest you read Coach Paula's book. If you've ever wondered how men decide who is "the one" for them, the answer can be found in *Why Won't He Commit?*

Coach Paula offers real life examples of women who have moved forward in their romantic life through coaching and have succeeded in capturing their Mr. Right. We don't want friends, sisters, moms, and even grandmothers wasting their time. Time and love are too precious to be wasted. You and the love you have to give are too precious to be wasted. Reading Coach Paula's book will help you in your search to find a committed partner who values you as much as we value you. With Coach Paula and The Rules, you will be valued by the men you meet and understand how, why, and when the right man will be "the one" to commit to you.

Ellen Fein and Sherrie Schneider
Authors of *The Rules*

Helpful Tips for Reading This Book

It's likely that you downloaded or picked up this book because you're with a man who is telling you he never wants to marry, is vacillating or giving you excuses regarding any type of commitment, or is simply avoiding the topic altogether. His love and desire to be with you is most likely quite apparent so you're baffled as to why he won't take things to the next level. You've wracked your brain and talked to all your friends about it. You've researched and read books, blogs, and articles. You may have even consulted a psychic or are waiting for Jupiter to align with Mars so that love steers your stars in the right direction. You're frustrated that there just don't seem to be any reasonable, logical, or even metaphysical answers. Why is he so resistant to commitment when it's clear he loves you and wants to be with you?

Why Won't He Commit? will give you the answer to this question and to many more that you may have about the behavior of men. You'll understand how men view, feel about, and commit to women, all from the perspective of a situation you've likely experienced in your own life. You will also come to understand the two states of being that men live in: one that allows a man to move forward in a committed relationship and one that does not.

In order to get the most you can from reading this book, I recommend that you read it through from cover to cover at least once without skipping ahead. As with many self-help books, there will be information and chapters in which you'll be most interested and wish to read right away. If you choose to jump around, make sure you read Chapter 3 before anything else. The information in this chapter is the foundation of *Why Won't He Commit?* Without having read the material in Chapter 3, subsequent chapters may be confusing, and you will miss references necessary to get the most from your reading.

From Night to Day, There is A Lot of Grey

All humans are on a scale of gender traits and characteristics. Some women are more stereotypically feminine than others and some men are softer and less stereotypically masculine than others. While there are certainly gender trait norms, variations are all within the broad spectrum of what can be considered normal, and there are always exceptions to every "rule."

If you were to think of human gender traits, behaviors, and characteristics as a series of points on a horizontal line drawn from left to right, the farthest left point on the line would be the utmost of stereotypical feminine traits. Think Marilyn Monroe. As you move to the right, each point on the line represents slightly more masculine qualities and ways of thinking, feeling, and behaving. The farthest point on the right of the line represents the utmost of stereotypical masculine qualities. Think Arnold Schwarzenegger.

GENDER SPECTRUM

Most
Feminine · · · · · · · · · · · · · · · Masculine

Generalized/Perceived Range of "Normal"

All of us have qualities, feelings, and traits of the opposite gender within us that are evoked and displayed at various times. Most of us fall somewhere within a range of what could be called the gender "norm" or what is typically expected according to gender "norms" in humans. It is within this range that I discuss the two genders related to ways of thinking, feeling, and behaving.

Every person is as unique as his or her fingerprints; however, *Why Won't He Commit?* stays within the middle range of the gender spectrum; that of "typical" male and female behavior. All that follows is written in the most broad and general of terms.

In almost every paragraph, you are likely to think of an exception to the "rule" regarding the situation being discussed or point being made. You'll be tempted to scoff at some of the points or concepts being presented as too generalized and dismiss the ideas altogether. While you will be right about the generalizations, check yourself when scoffing. Thinking of the exceptions will only keep you from getting the deeper meanings and salient points and ultimately the most value from your reading. It's important to absorb the concepts even though they are quite broad. This will allow you to see male behavior in its rawest form and help you to embrace it rather than question it or condemn it.

You are here because you want to understand men in a way you can relate to as a woman. The concepts in this book will do that for you if you let them. Reading from cover to cover once for the general concepts and then reviewing for specifics will help you connect what you've read to your own experiences. If you take the time to incorporate your reading into your life, the behavior of the men in your life will become clearer and perhaps even a little endearing.

Introduction

It's 2:00 am and you are lying in bed wide-awake. You pretend to be as asleep as the man with his back to you softly snores. Just a few hours ago, you were in the throes of rapture in this man's arms, receiving every ounce of his body and connecting in ways for which there are no words. Now, you are equally as uneasy and anxious as you were earlier enraptured. The wrestling between what your heart feels and what your head tells you is confusing, draining, and anxiety-provoking.

You can hardly close your eyes without recalling the smallest details of the previous week, month, or year with this man. How you've subtly pushed him, pursued him, or hinted for him to tell you how he feels and what he wants, only later to pull back and try to distance yourself and appear aloof. Replaying the movie in your mind of your many advances and retreats haunts and torments you.

While the man in deep sleep beside you doesn't give anything of himself, he always returns. His resistance is just fear, you think, as he is a good man and has shown you moments and glimpses of an ability to care about and love you. He's there in body so you believe he must be there in spirit, or he would have left. Will he become your husband (or even boyfriend), or is tonight the last time you will see him?

* * * * *

You and your guy are enjoying yet another weekend of bliss. Friday night was a movie and lots of easy conversation, fun, cuddling, and great sex. On Saturday, you woke up late, went to the gym together, and then he helped you shop for groceries and prepare a nice meal complete with wine and music. You talk about anything and everything. You feel that you're really connecting. You love being with him and developing this relationship.

A few hours out with your friends watching the game on Saturday night leads to sleeping late on Sunday morning, lounging, more sex, and the *Sunday Times* with lattes. When he leaves that afternoon or evening there is the usual "I'll talk to you soon" with lots of kissing and holding each other at the door. Three days later, you still haven't gotten so much as a text.

* * * * *

Your boyfriend of three years is deemed "a catch" by all who know him. He's fun, funny, smart, and industrious. When you look around at your friends, you can't believe how lucky you are to have such a committed and monogamous man by your side. He talks of the future and paints verbal pictures of how your life together might look "one day." He professes his love and on each special occasion you secretly hope to be getting a ring, yet it never comes. You try hard to make things good for him and prove yourself to be wife and mother material. You're beginning to think there is something about you that he questions for the long term. You are sick of waiting and your clock is ticking. When is he going to see that you two are meant to be husband and wife?

* * * * *

From the moment you met your man, you knew there was something different about him. He pursued you respectfully and has always made you feel special and wanted. You have never questioned his feelings, and things have always been easy, albeit a bit boring at times, as you have never felt that burning desire that other men have made you feel. You broke up briefly when a new hottie at work sparked the flame in you again, but when you realized how stupid you had been and begged Mr. Right for forgiveness, he took you back. Since then, you've devoted yourself to this great guy and have felt closer and more interested in him than ever.

You thought everything was back to the way it was, but it's been a year and Mr. Right hasn't popped the question. He is still wonderful, but he is beginning to show signs of distancing himself. You're afraid that you've ruined your chances at the one relationship that could have been forever. Why won't he commit?

Mirror, Mirror

Do you recognize yourself in any of the scenarios above? Depending on your love life, you may actually have experienced all four of them in one way or another. If so, you are not needy, damaged, or in any way anything other than the beautiful female that you were born to be.

What you've experienced with men – or perhaps are experiencing currently – is as normal and natural as the sun rising in the east and setting in the west, the birds and the bees, night and day, sun and rain, yin and yang, or male and female. You'll notice in this list of opposites that "good" and "bad" are not in the group. This is because men being men and women being women is not good or bad – it just is.

Understanding Nature Helps Us Nurture

Knowing and accepting that there are fundamental, biological, and anthropological reasons that men view things more in black and white rather than the contextual grey in which women tend to see things can help lessen your frustrations and allow you to do what you, as a woman, are uniquely equipped to do: understand, have patience for, and lovingly attend to the differences in people and living things.

Science has been able to address the debate over nature versus nurture and is now able to show us through neuro-brain imaging that nature is the full sundae of our experience, and nurture – or what we think of as socialization – is merely the cherry on top.

New research is confirming what humans have known since they developed higher thinking: there are slight differences in how the male and female brain are wired to behave and relate to their environment and other living beings. These slight differences, however, are akin to being from different planets; perhaps planets as different and as far apart as Mars and Venus.

The brain differences of men and women help account for the interconnected ways in which females are able to view people, problems, and emotional issues, and why males tend to look at things in more confined and linear ways. The way the male brain is wired is why it is largely a waste of time to try to get a man to view or understand emotional things in the same way that you do.

Males show stronger front to back wiring within each hemisphere of the brain, accounting for their greater spatial skills, motor coordination, and ability to visualize three-dimensional objects from various angles. Think Mr. Mechanic. Mike Mechanic is all about connecting parts and wires in order to problem-solve and get your car running. He is not apt to want to hear your tale of woe about your highway mishap and missing a big interview.

Although Mike might stand there and listen with a bit of a blank stare while you cry for a moment and recount the terror of losing all power while doing seventy-five miles per hour in the left lane, he's not likely to sit down with you or offer tissues and words of understanding. He is most interested in getting information so that he can set about problem-solving and fixing your car. This is his job. But, which comes first, the fact that he is a mechanic – so he is more interested in how parts of a car fit together than attending to your feelings – or that he is a man and his brain wiring is very well-suited for his job as a mechanic as opposed to a grief counselor? Likely a bit of both.

The Ewes Have It

Women have a slightly larger and fattier corpus callosum – the band of tissue that sits atop the brain and connects the two hemispheres. This allows for the two hemispheres of the female brain to speak to each other in a way that male brains don't as readily or as easily. Think Mrs. Mom. Margie Mom has to problem-solve in all manner of both tangible and emotional ways. Margie attends to the gash in her kid's knee while simultaneously getting his bike out of the road and stopping her other kids from stepping out in traffic. What she also does, so well and so easily, is assuage the fear all the children feel when their brother almost veers into oncoming traffic.

Rams Aren't Necessarily Dodging

Remembering that a man's ability to process and access emotions is somewhat slower for some men and seemingly non-existent for others will not only allow you to be more patient but will eventually allow you to fully embrace men in a way that you may have been fighting. While your situation will vary according to the uniqueness of your own brain and the brain of any man you're attempting to understand and communicate with, knowing what you are about to discover in the pages that follow will help you more than anything else: Men are wired to *love, commit, and bond* differently than women.

Despite their protests and aversion to "drama," men actually love what is different about women and find the deep emotions of women to be alluring, attractive, and enticing. This doesn't mean men will understand or even care to attempt to understand women, as understanding and connecting to differences is not inherently male; therefore, it's incumbent upon women, with their enhanced ability to understand and connect to others, to communicate and relate to men in ways that provide the best outcomes and chance of success in romantic relationships.

Tarzan and Jane, Not Jane and Jane

While we might wish men were emotionally more like us than different, would we really want that wish to come true? Likely not. It is in the differences between the sexes that we experience that special spark of chemistry, sexual attraction, and romantic love. Though not easy to navigate, it does make life passionate and fascinating, albeit at times heartbreaking, if not profoundly frustrating. Yet, without clouds, the rays of the sun would not feel as delightful as they do when they break through and warm us. Without night, there is no day. While things might be easier at times, they would not be as exciting and wondrous without men! And let's face it, traversing the jungle with their linear brains (and muscles) makes swinging on the vine of life more fun and many times a heck-of-a-lot easier!

My Learning Curve Balls

Perhaps there are women born with an innate knowledge and understanding of men, but it is my belief that they are a very fortunate few. Women born before the sexual revolution and women's movement were forced to adhere to socially accepted norms and behaviors which catered to men's natural need to be challenged, compete, and achieve that which they deemed worth achieving. As women began attaining political, social, educational, and professional equality to some degree, they did not naturally fare as well when it came to attaining committed relationships.

As a young girl, I erroneously believed that men and women were as equal in their relationships, the ways they loved, and in their needs and desires. Not having brothers and being more than a little sheltered and naïve, at barely seventeen years old, I left my small-town home for the very big city of New York. Thrust into adult city life, I found the world of men to be confusing at best, and at worst, almost entirely unforgiving and unyielding to female needs beyond the sexual.

Being exceedingly independent and fairly adventurous, I placed myself on an equal footing with men and did not account for the inherently different ways in which men and women love, attach, commit, and bond. While smart and savvy in many arenas of life, in the circus of love and relationships, I was the clown.

Fast forward several decades, and I am quite grateful to be out from under the Big Top and no longer walking in big floppy shoes donning a bright red nose. I did my time getting pies in my face and feeling like I earned a PhD in love from Clown College. My experiences with men was at times a three-ring circus. From short and tall, light and dark, outgoing and introverted, nerdy and artistic, weak-willed and strong-willed, narcissistic and humble, handsome and average, all who crossed my winding romantic path taught me about the minds and hearts of males. No textbook, courses, early training, or role modeling could ever have equaled the learning I received through my experiences.

Despite the pain and heartache, I'm grateful for all the good and not-so-good men in my life – from those who had no investment in me for more than the moment to the few who did and to the one I was smart enough to return the formal commitment he was ready, willing, and able to give. Alas, the universal circus of love and romance has provided me with a diverse education and wealth of experience. If not for all the joys, triumphs, confusion, and suffering, I would lack the knowledge I possess in the way I possess it, as well as the ability to understand the unique relationship situations and myriad circumstances my clients face in their romantic lives.

I continue to give thanks for the men in my life both past and present, as each one has contributed to this book in some form and has afforded me the opportunity to formally help and support the most giving creatures and caretakers of the world – women! The way in which women share their individual and collective experiences – giving of themselves to help their fellow sisters – is unparalleled in the male world, and I am happy to be a part of that sisterhood.

Don't Join the Club, But Do Support the Members!

We've all heard the adage, "If you can't beat 'em, join 'em." No need to worry. What you are about to read will not have you suddenly craving a cigar, wanting to get under the hood of a car for hours, or gambling on fantasy football. It also won't solve all your problems with the day-to-day annoyances of men not hearing you, understanding you, or attending to your needs in the myriad ways you attend to theirs.

What this book will do is give you valuable insights and allow you to begin to see men more objectively. It will provide you with several concepts and principles explaining how men communicate, view women, love them, commit, and bond. It will also provide you with information to find out where your man is on the scale of being ready, willing, and able to commit.

Through reading this book, you will begin to accept men as male and different – not wrong, bad, or unfeeling. Most importantly, the content of *Why Won't He Commit?* will empower you to know and feel how much you are loved by men just for being female and that you are truly desired for more than just your body. Whether you are big or small, short or tall, young or old, slim or ample, blond or brunette, prim or goth, dark or light, you are actually adored and loved by almost all men in one form or another almost all of the time. You will also begin to understand that male love will never be quite like your more magnanimous female love. By accepting and incorporating the information in this book, you can finally let go of the expectation that men will love in the same fashion or degree as women. You will start to free yourself to live the fullest and happiest romantic life possible.

If you're reading this book because you've been disappointed, hurt, confused, and/or angered by a man's inability to commit to you – despite years of devotion, love, and complete and utter commitment – The Puppy Principle in Chapter 3 will explain why this has happened to you and why it happens to women around the world no matter their age, beauty, height, race, religion, education, wealth or sophistication.

The Puppy Principle will help you to step into the hearts and minds of men through an experience you currently have, or have had, yourself. By grasping this principle, you will be able to feel what a man feels and understand what causes a man to forego great sex, a wonderful partner, a best friend, and a fabulous relationship – and not commit – even when he feels love for a woman.

The Consumer vs. Buyer Relationship Concept in Chapter 4 presents the two states of being that are inherent in adult men and determine when, why, and if a man will commit. In this section, the determining factors in each state are outlined and the needs every man must satisfactorily meet in order to be able to commit are clearly defined. It is here that you will come to understand that a man's capability and readiness to commit come from inside him and are only partially impacted by his love for a particular woman.

Pacing Yourself

When coaching my clients, I find myself reminding them to "think marathon and not sprint," meaning that they have to have patience with their own emotions and have patience with men being slow to trust that their emotions are more than sexual or fleeting. While initially showing infatuation, men cannot be expected to connect to a relationship in the same way women do.

The Puppy Principle will illustrate why a man is so readily affectionate and why he can show intense levels of interest initially and in the moment, only to be easily distracted by another woman the next.

Male and female time frames are very different in terms of relationships and sex; therefore, rushing any dating experience into a relationship will decrease a man's interest. Fast-tracking any relationship, no matter the chemistry, passion, or how interested a man appears, takes away the most important factor that allows him to completely fall in love: *the act of continually having to prove himself worthy and capable of achieving your time, attention, and affection.* I often remind my clients to "think sports," because for a man, no trophy or pennant that is easily won is as prized or valued as when it is a real challenge to attain.

For now, let's focus on what you have come here to learn: understanding how, why, and under what conditions a man will be ready, able, and most of all, willing to commit!

Chapter One
If It's Still So Early, Why Does It Feel So Late?

"I've been dating since I was fifteen, I'm exhausted...
where is he already?"

Although that famous line was uttered nearly two decades ago by the fictional character Charlotte in the HBO series *Sex and the City,* it continues to capture the feelings of real women everywhere. Increasingly, women of all ages and from all walks of life find themselves emotionally depleted from the difficulties associated with men and the failed attempts at having committed and lasting relationships.

Real-world Charlottes, Carries, and Mirandas are baffled at men's resistance to locking down love. While all the women on the show eventually made it to the altar (with even the commitment-phobic Samantha ultimately marrying), women in the real world find themselves struggling simply to find and date a nice guy who can maintain a relationship and commit to it!

In 2017, real women who are a decade older than the thirty-somethings in the television series are now dealing with the same issues the fabulous foursome did in the late 1990s and early 2000s. Statistically and realistically, women in their mid-to-late-thirties, as well as those in their forties and beyond, will find it a bit harder to find mates than the frolicking, fantasy femme-fatale four. *Sex and the City's* final episode was in 2004, and a great deal has socially changed since then. Those women nearly missed the online dating explosion and wouldn't have even heard of a thing called a dating app or "swiping right."

According to the last survey taken by the United States Census Bureau in 2016, there were 88 unmarried (single) men for every 100 unmarried (single) women in the United States. This statistic is for adult men and women across the lifespan from age eighteen to death, so it goes without saying that the number of available men vary depending upon age. The statistic also doesn't take into account the percentage of single men who are gay (21%), thus skewing things more in favor of single straight men looking for straight women.

In the last twenty years, women have also begun to outnumber men in terms of higher education. *The Boston Globe* reports that in 2014, female college/university enrollees were 55% female and 45% male. Higher female enrollment was a trend reported as early as the 1970s. It is a trend that has only risen over time and is expected to continue. Furthermore, with only 27% of unmarried adults twenty-five years and older getting college degrees, educated women are further limiting themselves should they wish to have an equally educated male partner.

Why the less-than-exciting statistics? Well, knowledge is power! Knowing that the odds are a bit against you in any endeavor is important as it can help direct your thoughts, expectations, and actions. When it's a seller's market in any field – whether it be real estate or what is known in the dating world as the "meat market," - most of the time a female buyer has to adjust her expectations for the best chance of finding a mate.

In terms of men, metaphorically speaking, that new luxury five-bedroom, four bath penthouse with a spectacular view is likely to be immediately snatched up by the highest bidder the moment it becomes available, maybe even before being put on the market.

With statistics as they are, women are significantly limited by the male inventory available, especially in cities where women outnumber men. It is up to you – the buyer in this analogy – to make the tough decisions about whether or not to *rent* while waiting for your *dream home* or opt to *buy* something more *modest* that is actually available and in which you can invest for the long term. While a bit *overpriced* when it becomes available – with cracks in the plaster and weeds all over the lawn – a bit of a *fixer-upper* of an available guy who is not in the best location could actually be a good investment for a lifetime of committed love.

Listen to Kenny Rogers

Watch Kenny Roger's video of *The Gambler* and listen to the chorus. The only lyric missing from that song is about actually knowing your odds. The fact that the odds are a bit against you shouldn't make you give up and throw in your chips but rather ensure that you know the rules of the game. In poker, as in dating and relationships, knowing how your opponent thinks dramatically increases your odds of winning and makes the game more enjoyable as well as less stressful. Undertaking a romantic relationship with anyone is always a huge gamble. Good odds or not, knowing when to "hold 'em, fold 'em, walk away, or run" is key to winning in the game of love and romance.

Playing smart and playing the odds starts with looking at where you live. It begins with online searching for the male-to-female adult and unmarried (single) ratio in your city or town. Don't forget to account for the roughly 21% of gay men, and you'll have a close approximation to your odds. The older you are, the more the figure is skewed in favor of men by approximately twenty to one, but that is if you're ninety years old! Again, accounting for gay males, those aren't odds most of us will want to be dealing with, but at ninety, if all one is thinking about is finding a guy – hey, life is pretty darned good! For those who are quite a bit younger, the odds are quite a bit better. Want to put the odds even more in your favor? Move to any city in Alaska or to Silicon Valley where it has been reported that there are as many as seven men to every three women.

Luck Be a Lady

It's one thing to know your odds, but it's more important in the dating world to make your own luck. Born in 4 BC, the philosopher Seneca is known for his saying, "Luck is what happens when preparation meets opportunity." Fortunately, for a woman in 2017, there are more ways than ever before to be prepared and to put luck on your side.

I know that the odds are in your favor because you are reading this book. That tells me that you're a woman who wants to know all that you can about men and what it takes to gain committed love and a fulfilling relationship.

If you're reading *Why Won't He Commit?* because you're wondering why your guy hasn't committed to you or why you have lost at love in the past, fortune has brought you to this table. By reading on, you have the best odds of winning. If there is not a specific guy, or you just plain haven't ever sat at the roulette wheel of romance, then you've also come to a great place to understand men and increase your luck!

Whatever your current circumstances – whether you're in a serious relationship or merely dating – viewing your opportunities positively is going to have an impact on your success. Men almost always view their opportunities with women positively. In this instance, men have got it all right! The fact is if you want to meet someone new, it's as easy as going out tonight where there are men and smiling at them!

Once a man you are interested in arrives in your life, you want to be sure (as any savvy gambler will remind you) to know how the man sitting across from you thinks and reacts at every turn in "the game."

Positive Spins!

Why Won't He Commit? is going to help you know a lot more than just your odds with men. It will help you from the most valuable vantage point – that of your "opponent" – from here on in referred to as your man, your guy, your lover, your fiancé, and hopefully, your husband! The knowledge you will gain from reading this book and getting professional guidance to ensure the man you desire will love and want you in return is fundamental. Together our goal is for you to know how "the game" is played and how best to read your "opponent." By understanding the principles that follow, you will understand that at the roulette table of romance, you don't want to squander your hard-earned opportunities!

If you are nearing the age of thirty-five and know you want to have children, now is the time to make your love life a priority! Having coached many women in their forties who are saddened by their missed opportunities to have their own biological children, I know the pain that postponing childbearing can cause. Whether or not you have a desire for children, as you near the age of forty and certainly beyond, you are wise to make your romantic life as much of a priority as your career or professional life. In short, carpe diem!

According to brainmeasures.com, for women ages forty to fifty, the chances of marriage are anywhere from just under 13% to just over 35% depending on the woman's exact age. The site has what they call a *chances to get married calculator* as well as an *after the age of forty calculator*. I love this tool because a woman's belief that she will marry is included in the calculation of her odds of success. It factors in that secret component of a *belief* in a desired outcome and assigns it a large role in the achievement of a dream.

Continuing to have a positive attitude through the inner knowing that you will be able to manifest and have the romantic life partner that you desire and deserve, is, and will be, a large part of your success. Another piece of the puzzle is knowing, understanding and relating to how men think, feel, commit, and bond.

What's Inside that Beautiful Package?

Where are you with your state of inner knowing? Are your beliefs firm because you are in a great place of always working towards self-actualization? Are they strong because you are committed to be the best person you can be, both inside and out? Are you in a committed relationship with a man you love, who cherishes you, and you both have mutual positive regard that allows you to get through each day with hope, happiness, and wholeness, or have you been through the mill with men? Are you all tussled and torn-up by a haunting group of past lovers or dates who left you heartbroken, confused, hardened or just plain numb?

Most every woman has her own positive and negative past experiences that both bolster her self-esteem and haunt her at times. The haunting may come from a failed marriage or several boyfriends that weren't right, possibly including a wonderful man who gave you the world, but you simply didn't love enough to stay with for a lifetime. Was there a charming jerk who treated you like yesterday's newspaper over whom you kick yourself for ever having given the time of day? Chances are, because you're a woman, you have given your all to every man with whom you were involved. And because you are human, you did the best you knew how to do at the time.

While there might be quite a few lovers-past, the memory of them needn't haunt you. By reading this book, you will see that all the giving, connecting, compromising, and caretaking you did – while making sense from your female way of loving and committing – likely had the opposite effect of what you intended and lessened the desire and love of some of the men in your past.

It's Really Not You, It's Him and You Together!

Using the principles in this book, you will come to see that to a great extent what happened in your failed relationships had little to do with you and almost everything to do with the fact that men and women feel and express love in very different ways. This lack of understanding and acceptance of the different needs, wants, styles, and ways of loving, communicating, committing, and bonding are the cause of the complex difficulties men and women face in their relationships with each other.

While we'd like to think we "grow apart" or just have "irreconcilable differences," statistics point to the fact that gender differences could be the primary factor in divorce.

The Netherlands' Central Bureau of Statistics found that in the fifteen years since the country passed marriage equality, same-sex couples have boasted a lower divorce rate overall than straight couples. Recent research from the Williams Institute at UCLA Law School, lends credence to the fact that same sex relationships (where brains are more similarly wired), "showed a breakup rate [that] is about half of what it is among their heterosexual counterparts."

Winning the War of the Sexes

In his book, *The Problem with Women...Is Men: The Evolution of a Man's Man to a Man of Higher Consciousness*, author and self-proclaimed recovering playboy, Charles J. Orlando, lauds his wife for making him the man he has become. It is interesting to note that even with its catchy title, this book did not become a phenomenal hit like *The Rules*. Perhaps this is because Mr. Orlando's premise that women have no need to alter their behavior to make relationships work flies in the face of what women grow to understand: that their natural giving and loving inclinations towards men are not usually what men respond to most positively.

Charles Orlando is under the assumption that his wife did little to inspire him to change his playboy ways. I daresay that Mr. Orlando likely had no idea of the strategies and approaches his wife was invoking in their dating (and most likely invokes to this day) in order to continually ignite and inspire her husband's interest and desire. Mrs. Orlando may be one of those lucky women who innately knows and lives by adage #1 on my List of Gender Gaps:

Women Love Through Knowing; Men Love Through Wondering.

#1 of Coach Paula's List of Gender Gaps

I have no doubt that Mrs. Orlando keeps her husband wondering in all the little ways that keep his interest alive, and thus propels him to continually behave and act in ways that make her happy and feeling loved, cherished, and desired. Though she may be doing so unconsciously, if Mr. Orlando is so enamored that he wrote a book, I know his wife is doing the work! More on that work in later chapters. For right now, let's focus on you and your understanding of men.

Naughty or Nice

Take a moment to think about all the men in your life, past and present. Get a piece of paper or pull out your phone and make a list that includes all the men you've either dated a few times, seriously dated, or with whom you had significant relationships – long or short, good or bad, pretty or ugly. List them all and don't limit yourself. If you recall someone and think, "Ugh, I couldn't stand that guy," he goes on the list!

If you have any resistance to doing this exercise, let those feelings wash over you and connect to them. What are those feelings about? Denial, shame, regret? It's okay. Lovers past are now just names on a piece of paper or a list on your phone's notepad.

Next, circle or highlight the name or names of the men that you loved or were deeply infatuated with *at the time.* Just think about how you felt *at the time, without judging yourself.* Do this according to your feelings then and not with hindsight. There is no need to think, "We were from such different backgrounds, it never would have worked," or "I barely knew him!" Just go with how you felt about him when you were with him.

It's likely that you will have circled all but one or two of the men on your list because at the time you were together, you loved him or were, at the very least, infatuated with him. For the serious and long-term relationships, it's likely that you loved each man so much that you would have given anything to be with him despite his flaws or problematic behavior. You were committed to him, heart and soul, regardless of the length of the relationship, the distance between you, or other mitigating factors.

Now go down the list, one by one, and put a heart next to the men who loved you back to an equal extent, or who loved you regardless of whether or not you loved them. Finally, go down the list again, this time putting an X next to the men who – whether you knew it at the time or only now recognize – did not love you. Try to put yourself in the mind and heart of each one – not what you would have wanted or what is less painful to think about or remember.

That icky guy you eventually couldn't stand – did he get a heart or an X? The man who you thought was "the one" but who shattered your heart into a million pieces – did he get a heart and an X? In looking at the list, what do you notice? How many names were both circled or highlighted *and* had the heart next to them? How many were circled or highlighted and had an X next to them? How many simply had an X?

Bodies of Water

A woman's love is like an ocean. When a woman stands at the shore and looks at the horizon, she is totally open to the sea and the vastness of blue water. She dips her toes in the surf to test these waters. If they are warm and inviting, and she likes the way the water feels, she ventures out a bit farther.

Having sex causes the tides to turn as a woman is carried out into a deeper part of the sea. The longer she is with a man and continues to have sex with him, the deeper and deeper her feelings become until those feelings carry her leagues under the deepest part of the ocean, nearing the depths of the sandy floor.

A man's love is more like a lake than an ocean – and by lake, we're not talking the Great Lakes! A man can see across this shallower, smaller body of water. As he ventures out across it, his lake is not as deep, and it doesn't just "drop off" to depths unknown. A man also doesn't generally care to test the water; instead, he just dives in. If he likes how it feels and it's not too murky, rough, or filled with crocodiles or other biting creatures, he'll continue to walk across the lake without much thinking. Early on, he finds that it drops to its deepest level, but it often doesn't take him "under." The depth of his "body of water" remains at about the same level until he nears the shore on the other side.

When a man has sex with a woman, nothing much changes in terms of how he feels about the woman other than the desire to pursue her to have more sex. The waters stay at the level at which they began. If they are deep, it is because he felt something genuine and real. They will remain deep. If shallow, it is because there were no other feelings except the desire to pursue for sex. They will remain shallow. After having sex, a man's feelings generally stay much where they started.

It's important to make the distinction that a man's continued desire to have sex has *nothing* to do with his feelings. If a man isn't crazy for you when he first has sex with you, he won't become more so as he "walks across the lake." Conversely, even if he was crazy for you in the beginning, if you "pull him under" with the depth of your "ocean" of feeling too soon, he will likely fight to come up for air as he races across his "lake" to the other shore. It is then that he most likely runs for the hills in fear of being "drowned" by your emotions.

In your past relationships, perhaps you moved somewhere you didn't particularly want to live or gave up your ideal career position so that you could be with your man more. Perhaps you changed your work schedule, regular hobbies, or meetings with friends and family in order to accommodate his schedule. To the degree that you loved, you were likely willing to do anything that you felt would connect you and keep you in a loving relationship. Unfortunately, while you believed your compromises would help your man see you as the giving, loving creature you are, and thus love you more, it likely did little to inspire him in the way a man needs inspiration to experience feelings of love and desire.

If you now regret having done anything in your past, know that your actions likely came from a place of loving and wanting to connect and caretake. Loving and giving is fully and beautifully female and is deserving of male love and devotion in return for all that you are, all that you do, and all that you will do again when given the chance.

The key to being successful in love is to inspire a man in the way he experiences love *from the start*. Love can actually be invoked quite easily in a man, via a woman creating *wonder* and *longing* in him from the very first meeting. To fan the flames of love and desire, a woman must keep wonder alive in small, subtle, and consistent ways.

You Are Love

If I were sitting beside you right now, we could go down the list you made earlier. After asking just a few questions about each guy, I would be able to tell you whether he actually loved you or not. To your surprise, with very few exceptions, I would be telling you that he did love you to one degree or another!

You knew you were loved by the men you were in serious relationships with when you were told you were loved *and* when the men behaved in a manner congruent with their words. You felt their love through feeling safe, secure, and trusting. In short, through *knowing*!

Because men feel love, experience love, and express it differently, you were likely loved by most all the men in your past to one degree or another – either for a night, a month, or one or two decades! Some of the love you've received from men came at a time in their lives when they were not ready, willing, or able to commit to a woman despite their feelings. This may be very hard for you to understand because, as a woman, you connect love to commitment and bonding in a way that men do not.

Neither love nor time is much of a factor in men being ready, willing, and able to commit. Your lack of having a commitment now, or in the past, is almost assuredly not because you are not, or were not, loved in some way. It's simply that you lack the skill of recognizing the state of being a man *must* be in, in order to make a decision to commit.

Once you understand this state and learn how to recognize it, you will not only save time, but you will know that you are rarely the cause of a man not wanting to commit to you.

At the End of the Tunnel

You have come to this book at this time in your life for a reason. You are a thinker and a seeker and know that there are answers for those who choose to take action. Congratulate yourself for taking that kind of action! The principles here, alongside other resources and chances for on-going support, will help you make small adjustments in your way of thinking, relating, and communicating with men. Helped along by several concepts, strategies, and approaches, your desire and willingness to educate yourself already sets you on a path toward success, commitment, and long-term happiness!

Connecting to Your Own State of Being

You know there are ways to improve your romantic life and have the committed relationship every woman deserves; however, frustration can cause internal strife and self-doubt – especially if a desire for children is involved.

As self-doubt can turn inward to depression, it's easy to see why it becomes vital to have support at every step on the path to finding Mr. Right and having him commit. Unfortunately, most women tend to turn to readily available help in the form of their friends, ads that pop up on social media, catchy headlines on magazines at the checkout counter, astrologers, and even psychics. Whether it's the hot selling headline of the moment, the ad that scrolls by, or the tarot card that is turned over, women are constantly given advice that is completely antithetical to what is useful for them to actually succeed with men.

Women are often hurt more than helped by the well-meaning advice of others. When in an emotional situation, subjective advice from friends can seriously lessen a woman's chances of gaining a committed relationship. Objective, strategic, and trained expert help is the most useful in helping women attain success in the committed relationships they desire and deserve.

Chapter Two

Getting Down to the Nickie-Gritty

One of my clients, whom I'll call Nickie, started working with me at the age of forty-two. She was a ruby-haired beauty from the northeast who, while free-spirited and artsy, held a great job in the tech industry. She had recently bought her first home and felt ready to start the next chapter of her life.

Nickie came to me seeking my Commitment Clarity program. Because I only work with women who are totally committed to getting what they want in their romantic lives, I questioned why she was coming to me at this particular time in her life. She reported that she had recently begun to research the medical and legal options to have a baby on her own. While working on the possibility of adoption, she was also investigating having her own child through a sperm donor. Nickie wanted to work with me regarding the men she was dating so that she would have the best possible chance of having a child naturally. She stated that she knew she needed to prioritize her desire for commitment in a way she had not done before, and this showed me that she was serious. She had recently read about how I had helped a woman in her mid-forties go from online dating to engaged in less than a year, and she wanted the same results.

Upon hearing her high level of commitment and wanting to help her achieve her personal goal, I took Nickie on for coaching and we began to work together. She reported that she was meeting men both online and off who were typicall educated, successful, and in their late thirties and early forties. She was dismayed that "nothing was gelling" for her with the exception of one man she described as "very sexy."

Nickie impressed me as smart, achieved, and goal-oriented. She was also kind and had a lot of social and artistic interests. She had a serious boyfriend all through college in upstate New York and, upon graduating, went directly to graduate school in Boston. Her boyfriend decided to take a job in northern California however, so the couple had a long-distance relationship. Nickie planned on moving out west once she completed her master's degree, but the relationship ended in heartbreak when she discovered that her "committed" boyfriend had been seriously seeing the human resources director at his new job.

In the three to four years following the breakup, Nickie had a series of short-term relationships and a variety of dating experiences. It wasn't until nearly five years later, at the age of twenty-nine, that Nickie got into her next long-term relationship with Ken. The two had a solid relationship and lived together for nearly seven years.

Early on, Nickie had doubts about Ken ever wanting to marry or have a family. When his mother was diagnosed with a serious illness, Nickie said that she "didn't want to press" the issue of marriage. Once it was known that Ken's mother would survive, and he showed no signs of wanting the relationship to move forward, Nickie ended it. After that, Nickie reported a lull in her dating life, followed by several "flings" mixed in with a few serious, short-lived relationships that "almost always" left her heartbroken.

Nickie decided that she was no longer willing to wait for a committed relationship and would try to have a child on her own. While she wasn't going to give up on finding Mr. Right, she was looking at having a relationship as a means to an end that she desired, along with several "other possibilities," as she put it. "Besides," she declared, "I want to be with a man regardless."

As an avid skier and amateur photographer, Nickie had a very full social life and was meeting a few men organically. To increase her dating options and possibilities, she had recently joined several online dating sites.

Online dating presented a unique challenge for Nickie. She wanted to have an honest and as straightforward a profile as possible, yet she felt that if she put her real age of forty-two, along with a desire for marriage and children, she would be scaring off men who might otherwise want to meet her. Nickie's approach did not seem to be geared toward easy success. She was very reluctant to miss out on any opportunities and felt she couldn't take herself off the dating sites until she figured out exactly what was going to happen in terms of the pregnancy that she touted as her main goal.

Nickie looked very young for her age so claiming that she was thirty-six years old never raised any suspicion from the men that she attracted online; however, not being completely truthful weighed heavily on her, especially when a man showed more than just a passing interest. Nickie felt that in terms of online dating and her profile statement of wanting children, she had no choice but to put a younger age on her profile. She felt that prospective men who did not know her would deem her real age and desire to have children as a serious limiting factor. Unfortunately, this caused Nickie to be in constant worry about when to tell a man the truth. Most importantly in terms of her success, this worry kept her from totally being herself in the dating process.

Nickie rationalized that if a man fell in love with her first, she could then tell him the truth about her age. She felt she could also then tell him the truth about her plan to have a child, whether through adoption or with a man wishing to join her in the journey of parenting.

Since she had begun taking steps towards her goal of having a child, her life had become full of doctor's appointments and meetings with her lawyer, her financial advisor, and her accountant. She was also remodeling her new home.

Nickie soon told me more about the "very sexy" man she had seen a few more times, named Todd. She admitted that she was really starting to like Todd and that they shared an instant chemistry. Todd was thirty-nine years old and was briefly married for three years when he was in his mid-twenties. He told Nickie that he was tired of dating and wanted to settle down and perhaps even have a family. This was music to Nickie's ears, and she became very excited by the appropriate prospect that Todd appeared to be. While happy for her, I gently reminded her of one of my coaching mantras: *think marathon and not sprint*, especially when first getting to know a man.

Nickie took direction from our initial work on dating strategies and never reached out to Todd. I explained that any forward motion toward a man can cause him to lose interest and perhaps even retreat. Nickie realized the power of choosing to wait for Todd to text or call. She also applied another important strategy for heightening a man's interest: she didn't immediately reply to him when he contacted her, thus forcing him to wait and *wonder*.

Despite wanting to send little texts or answer immediately when he reached out, Nickie held back, and Todd responded by showing a lot of interest. Nickie also worked on keeping herself from asking Todd many questions during their initial dates, especially about his personal life or feelings. She allowed their dating to unfold at his pace and let him take the lead on asking questions and directing the discussion. This proved to be very challenging for Nickie on several levels. First, being a woman, Nickie connects through interactive discussion. Because men can perceive this kind of interaction as too much interest or pursuit, I coached Nickie to hold back on her natural inclination to ask questions and talk a lot. While talking makes women feel most connected, I explained how listening works best initially, as men tend to like to talk more "at" women in the first few dates to tout their achievements.

While different than what she was used to, this type of holding back proved advantageous for Nickie in her situation, as she was not comfortable with sharing much about herself with Todd for obvious reasons. She was lying about her age and didn't want to slip up and divulge any info on what she was planning. Furthermore, she had to be careful about the timeline of her life – like the year of her college graduation, the years that she was in high school, and when she had left home. Simply listening to Todd talk about his work, his hobbies, and his friends proved to be a bit of a relief for Nickie.

When Todd asked Nickie about herself, she handled her discomfort by diverting the conversation back to his life. Despite all of her positive reports on their dates, I sensed that her caution caused Nickie to seem less fun and spontaneous as I knew her to be.

The Power of "Not Yet"

Nickie also understood that waiting to have sex with a man allows him to experience falling in love in the most profound way a man can: by catering to his need to achieve and allowing him to wonder if and when he will succeed. Nickie was quite attracted to Todd so I made sure to remind her that men fall in love through a delay in gratification. I explained that when a simple "not yet" is implied in dating (it should not have to be said), it ignites a man's deepest need in life and in love, which is to wait to achieve what it is that he values and pursues!

When a woman employs the concept of "not yet," she takes a powerful stance. Men like to win, but more specifically, men like to win what they have spent their time and attention trying to achieve. When a woman holds off on having sex, even if a man knows that the woman also wants to have sex, she shows herself to be a woman of value – a trophy, prize, or pennant! In other words, a goal worthy of pursuit.

As we continued working together, Nickie uncharacteristically cancelled several of our scheduled sessions. By the next time we spoke, she had had two more dates with Todd. In just a few moments of catching up, I realized why Nickie had opted out of our previously set appointments. She was distressed over having had sex with Todd on the fourth date. She expressed disappointment in herself and concern that she had thwarted his ability to feel as deeply as he was potentially capable of feeling for her. She was now afraid that he was pulling away because not counting the one text he had sent the morning after, Todd had not reached out to Nickie in nearly a week.

The Good, the Bad, and the Scared

My heart went out to Nickie. She admitted that she felt increasingly anxious with each passing day that she didn't hear from

Todd. The high on which Nickie had been riding when Todd was pursuing her so heavily prior to their fourth date was now completely gone, and she was left with worry and doubt. Nickie confessed to me what made her feel "worst of all" was that she had had unprotected sex.

We explored why Nickie would put herself at risk, both emotionally and physically. Eventually, she was able to verbalize a number of feelings that were hard for her to come to terms with: that she was willing to risk causing herself harm because of her fear of not being able to get pregnant. While painful to admit, Nickie was making the connection that her fear was causing her to toss out her personal boundaries and safety concerns.

Nickie cried when she told me that she wasn't really ready to sleep with Todd and that despite our work together, her best friend had convinced her that she might lose Todd if she made him wait. Nickie confessed that the night before she met Todd for the fourth date, her friend told her that if she didn't sleep with him that night, he would "get tired of waiting" and likely not want to see her again.

We discussed why her friend's thinking was counter to what Nickie was looking to achieve in the long run, what she was feeling, and what she actually wanted to do physically. We also touched on the fact that acting from fear is in direct opposition to what men crave and what keeps them pursuing women that they like: their need to achieve and win that which is slightly out of reach.

Through Nickie delving more deeply into her feelings and actions, she realized that giving into her fear was pushing her to disregard not only all that we had achieved in our work up to that point, but also to abandon her own experience and inner knowing: that sleeping with a man is not a way to gain his real interest, and anything done with a man from a place of fear is destined to cause self-harm and probable heartache.

Nickie also admitted that despite the chemistry between her and Todd, the sex was "really awful." I helped her understand that because she was not comfortable with her decision, she was experiencing great dissonance between her mind, body, and heart. By giving into her fear and not adhering to her own desires, feelings, and values, she had forsaken herself and what she held in esteem. She was acting from a place of weakness and the effect was the polar opposite of her intention and desire.

Nickie also said she was feeling guilty about lying to Todd in the split second before they had sex when he asked if she was on birth control. "I don't know what came over me!" she lamented. "I told him I was!"

Nickie was distraught. She said she could not believe that she had "done it again!" When I asked her to explain, she recalled times in the past when she had used her sexuality in ways that she felt were working to her advantage. In reality, they simply brought her to a place of regret and emptiness, and she now saw clearly that her response to Todd was part of a pattern.

I was happy to be able to calm Nickie's fear of never hearing from Todd again, as I knew with 100% certainty that he would be reaching out to her, just not in the timeframe that she would have liked or felt would be most appropriate. I told her what I tell all of my female clients: take the amount of time *you* feel would be appropriate or normal in any given dating situation and *triple it*.

I explained to Nickie how we could work to reset her relationship with Todd and repair the bit of damage that had been done by sleeping with him before she was emotionally ready. I knew this would be hard for her, as it is the hardest of all strategies for most women because women connect sex to their feelings. In order to reset their relationship, Nickie was now faced with the difficult task of tempering her feelings and acting as if nothing had changed for her by having had sex.

In Nickie's particular case, I knew that the issue wasn't just Todd or what I call the "man of the moment" but rather, her real need and desire to connect to her feelings in order to make progress personally.

Connecting the Dots

In the next few months, I worked with Nickie to help her identify what she truly wanted for her life. First, she had to name it and claim it. Second, she had to focus on that one need, foregoing other easy, fun, and immediate distractions. Lastly, she had to commit to herself in a way that she hadn't in the past. Having a coach who was supportive and yet held her to her own choices, goals, and self-commitments helped her to identify, claim, and seek what she really wanted and needed, not what she thought she should want at her age or what she felt she should be doing.

What Nickie discovered was surprising to her, especially in the midst of what she had been attempting to undertake during the previous year. Nickie realized that in all the years since her first heartbreak with her college boyfriend, her deepest need and desire was being masked by what she deemed her promiscuity and flippant attitude and now by her focus on having a baby. Nickie uncovered that she wanted a committed, loving, and connected relationship with a man much more than she wanted to have a child.

Moving Forward

After Nickie finally admitted to herself that she would be desperately unhappy should she not find a life partner and only moderately disappointed if she didn't have a child, she freed herself to make finding a mate a priority and released herself from the pursuit, time, and pressure of getting pregnant, either artificially or naturally.

Other clients have been in similar situations to Nickie's and felt completely the opposite in terms of their desires. One former client in her early forties wanted a child more than anything else in her life. Through our time of working together, she discovered she didn't much care about finding the right relationship, but thought that having a man in her life would be the means to the end of being able to have a baby. Once she released herself from focusing on that which she didn't care about as much – a relationship – and started focusing on that which she deeply desired – having a child – she freed herself and started living a more satisfying, authentic, and goal-oriented life.

When Nickie identified that she truly desired a committed, monogamous relationship with a man she loved, she began accepting things as they were. She accepted her age and was okay whether or not she had a child. She discovered that with her main desire in complete focus, she could let go and allow fate to direct her path.

The Future in Now

Nickie and I continued to work together on the approaches and strategies necessary to ignite a man's interest by allowing him to love through wondering and by attempting to achieve her time, attention and affection. Nickie's focus of wanting a committed relationship keeps her steady on her path, so now she acts through strength and not fear. She removed her old, online profile and joined a site with her real age.

Todd did follow up with Nickie subsequent to their fourth date and Nickie worked with the strategies and approaches necessary to keep his interest in achieving her. Here are a few of the most important points and action steps that I have given to Nickie and are giving to you for the best chance of success with men:

1. **Don't Reach Out:** No matter how short, sweet, or
    innocuous a call or text initiated by a woman may

seem, they can lower a man's interest. While perhaps it's difficult for you to fully grasp, keep in mind that as much as you wish to be connected, a man's wish is to be independent and free to pursue that which he finds interesting. Take away that pursuit – even a little – and you can lessen a man's interest a lot.

2. **Don't Answer Quickly or Predictably:** Making a man wait for your answer is one of the best ways to pique his interest. Not answering a call or texting back right away, makes him think about you and question your interest in him. This small action spurs his achievement need, which is the deepest need for a man.

3. **Make Your Own Life Your Priority:** The value of showing a man that your life takes precedence over him cannot be overstated. While this doesn't mean that you never have any time for him, keeping a man off-balance in terms of where he stands in your list of priorities is important for him to be able to feel love for you.

Nickie wanted to confess to Todd that she had made a mistake by sleeping with him on the night of their fourth date, but I explained why that would not be a good idea. While there is much more to the reasoning behind this, the three basic guidelines are:

1. **Don't Go Back:** Stay in the moment with men. For men, the adage "that was then, this is now"

should always be in the forefront of your mind and interactions. Be true to yourself *in the moment* and do not bring up incidents from the past, unless specifically asked about them.

2. **Act, Don't Speak:** Women relate through verbalization, men relate through action. Don't tell a man that you are going to do something or why you are doing it; just do what you know to be best for yourself *in the moment*. If questioned, state that whatever you are doing is from your truth and your feelings about what is right for you, *right now*.

3. **Accept, Don't Acquiesce:** While you can appreciate a man's needs and wants, it doesn't mean you have to give into them. I often say these three little words to my clients to explain why they lose otherwise interested men: *You're too nice!* Stay strong in your own knowledge about what is right for you. Doing anything you don't want to do in order to "be nice" almost always backfires with men. Men aren't looking for women to be nice to them. Men are looking for women to be themselves and to inspire them to want to continually achieve their time, attention, and affection.

By following these tips, Todd remained interested in Nickie and was by all accounts intrigued by her. She went out with him again and stayed strong in what she did and did not want to do, sexually and otherwise. By her attending to her own feelings and knowing that attempts to please Todd did nothing to inspire his desire, she kept his interest. The two went on four more dates before Nickie had sex with Todd again, and this time she insisted on him using protection.

Without the pressure of the time constraint to get pregnant, Nickie began to view Todd just for Todd and her interest quickly fizzled. She felt that while he was "nice and sexy," the two had nothing in common and that their intellectual and recreational interests were very far apart.

Nickie is now dating someone new who appears to be a much better fit for her lifestyle and the two have a great deal in common. This man is a year older, has one child from a previous marriage, and said he is open to having another child "if it should happen." Nickie reports that she now feels at ease and how it is "ironic" that she has found a man with a child who might also become part of her life should the relationship become serious. She is now happier living in her greatest truth of desiring a committed relationship and focusing on making that happen.

Chapter Three
Puppy Love

When meeting someone new at a party, a social gathering, or an event, one person invariably asks about the profession of the other. It's a natural part of social interaction between relative strangers making conversation and, in some cases, actually trying to get to know one another. Depending on the circumstance, or to whom I'm talking, I either state that I'm a social worker or a dating and relationship coach. While the former generally ends the questioning rather quickly, the latter typically raises interest and further probing.

Many times, when talking with men, I often choose to tell them that I'm a dating and relationship coach. This allows me to gather lots of useful and honest answers to my questions. I think of it as fun, anecdotal research of sorts. Mostly, I am asked a lot of questions myself, so I have to be in the mood to talk about what I do for a living.

One such encounter happened while on a layover between flights from San Francisco to New York City. I was parked on a bar stool, catching up on emails, having a mediocre dinner with the totally disengaged bartender, while watching the 24-hour-a-day, political channel airing on the TV above. A man in his mid-to-late-thirties was seated next to me, and we somehow began discussing the latest media-inflamed story. When he asked what I did for a living, since I had nothing but time, I decided to be forthcoming. This traveler was instantly talkative and took it as his chance to make a few statements, some of them only slightly veiled as questions for which he wanted a female perspective.

One such statement (that luckily came after I had decided to order a glass of wine) took me aback at first. "I don't understand you women," he said. "Why wouldn't you just want to have sex all the time with any guy? You have the opportunity any time you want, with whoever you want, and it feels good, so why wouldn't you just do it? It doesn't make any sense to me!"

I didn't know if it was just the right amount of vodka that helped him voice his feelings with a female stranger, or if he truly didn't understand the inherent difference between men and women and was merely naïve or stupid enough to ask such a question in the blunt manner that he did. It didn't matter; he had voiced it. I was simply glad to have a glass of wine to pick up in that moment!

While it might be easy to immediately think of this airport stranger as a total bonehead, he was so sincere in the question that it was almost sad to witness him ask it. I could see that he was truly disheartened that the world of sexual interaction between the genders was so difficult and complex for women while for him it was simple and straightforward. From this man's point of reference, it really didn't make any sense that women, able to have exactly what he wants to have as a man, wouldn't take advantage of the ability to have it! He went on to paint a picture of how the world would be if women were, well, not women, but men.

I realized this man was simply voicing the frustration all men have at one time or another, or in some cases, all the time. This guy knew he would never see me again and didn't care that he came off as immature or idiotic. He just wanted to vent and felt that because I do what I do, I would not find anything he said about women to be mildly offensive or totally lacking in insight.

Entrapment

We are all trapped by our own experiences, none of which are quite as significant as those that happen because of our gender. While the man at the airport was an extreme example of a male unable to relate to the experience of being female, to one degree or another, we all have a bit of difficulty putting ourselves in the shoes of the opposite sex.

In my years as a coach for women, and also as a female with female family members and friends. it has been my experience that the greatest cause of women's heartbreak and pain comes from their inability to understand and accept how men view women, love them, make their decisions to commit to them, and bond. I thought that if I could somehow convey to women the way men experience women and love, I would be helping women not only to heal from their disappointments and losses a bit more easily, but also to feel much better about themselves and more confident in general. I also knew that in order for women to really get it, I would need to relay how men experience women through an experience that women have, or have had themselves. The Puppy Principle was born.

He's a Litter Bug!

Imagine for a moment that you are seriously considering getting a puppy of your own for the very first time. You happily research and find a breeder who you feel is going to have just the right pup to be your new love. You call the breeder who says, "You're in luck! About nine weeks ago we had three full litters so come on by and take your pick!"

You excitedly call one of your closest friends, Laura, who loves dogs as much as you do. She agrees to make the trip with you and you head to the breeder's home where you're warmly welcomed. Just walking in the door creates a feeling of excitement. The feeling grows with each step as Ms. Breeder escorts you to an adjacent playroom filled with seventeen frolicking little bundles of joy and pep. She tells you to take all the time you'd like, and she'll check in with you later.

You immediately drop to the floor to take in all of the adorableness, and Laura happily joins in. One puppy is cuter than the next, and you lose yourself in all the jumping, running, playing, and cuddling. You can't get enough of how cute they look, how soft their fur feels, and how their little ears smell like heaven. Even them nipping at your fingers with their little needle teeth endears them to you. While you are on the floor of that playroom, the world stops, and all your cares are gone!

You and Laura laugh and coo as you inhale the attention and innocent love you receive from these sweet creatures. You're on a lovely little high of sorts. Even when a pup that you want to hold runs away from you, it's fun to chase after it, pick it up, and sweetly scold it for not coming to you as you desire! It's all rainbows and cartwheels while in the presence of these little cuties.

That's His World

Welcome to the world of men and how they feel when in the company of women. How you feel with puppies, whether en masse with seventeen around you, one-on-one with a special cuddler, or chasing after a little imp who nips at you, you enjoy every minute of your experience with puppies.

Women are all "puppies" to men. They love us all. Big and tall, short and small, feisty and tame, or cuddly and illusive. From "Dachshunds" to "Great Danes," "Shih-Tzus" to "Shepherds," "Pit Bulls" to "Poodles," we are all endearing and appealing to men in one way or another. Just to be in our company feels engaging, comforting, relaxing, and fulfilling. Even when we nip at them, we are still intoxicating, interesting, alluring, and always visually stimulating to men.

Have you ever been out and walked by a cute dog? If you are a dog lover, you can't help but be visually drawn and may even exclaim, "Oh, how cute!" without even thinking before the words come out of your mouth. At the same time, you might have moved toward the pup to pet it, or let it jump on you with no thought of potential dirt or slobber. You don't know the doggie, but if it's friendly and affectionate, you'll find yourself embracing it, petting it, hugging it, and maybe even kissing it.

This is the same kind of feeling men experience when looking at women as they walk by. On the streets of crowded cities, certain men will "cat-call" to women. This is akin to how an exclamation of glee can't help but come out of you, at times, when you see a cute puppy. His whistle or "wow," "beautiful," or "sexy," simply comes out of him before he even thinks. Depending on the situation, the man, and the circumstances, it can either be flattering or offensive. Women question why men make remarks when women don't respond back. "What do they expect?" women ask me. "Do they really think I'm going to turn around and do something or say something back?"

Know that you are a pretty "puppy" when you walk by and get a whistle or remark. Just as there are times when an "Oh, how cute!" simply comes out of you when you see a puppy, this is what is happening with a man who verbally responds to you when you walk by.

If not for social mores and conventions, men would likely be making comments and gestures to women a great deal more than they do. In Italy, it's commonplace for men to touch women on the street. When out walking, men will touch women or even pinch them as they make a flirty remark. It's done "in fun," as in "boys will be boys." While waning in recent years, to Italians, this practice is a harmless display of men's appreciation for women that is still culturally accepted.

While you might be thinking that it is their sexual desire that provokes men to make remarks or whistle at women passing by, I say that you are partially correct. While there is a sexual component of the equation, it is smaller than you might imagine. It's more about an overriding *feeling* men have that encompasses all of their male being when they see the female form.

Think of how you can't take your eyes off a cute puppy or kitten, especially when you are in a relaxed state of mind and aren't distracted by something important. Then think of how it might be if, in addition to that attraction, there was a component of sexual interest. This is what it is like to be male. Pretty distracting, no?

You Don't Have to Be "Best in Show" or Even a Contender

Most of us are attracted to one breed of dog over another. Perhaps you prefer Beagles to Boxers or Bulldogs to Bichons, but if you like dogs, almost all breeds will be in some way appealing to you either in looks or temperament. A gentle giant of a Rottweiler that is the sweetest dog you've ever encountered appeals to your heart. A snorting, bug-eyed Pug is so loving you can't help but want to protect it from the world. Ever heard the expression, "It's so ugly, it's cute?"

While men have the "breed" or "breeds" they prefer, all women are appealing, attractive, or endearing to them in one way or another. How many times have you said or heard "What does he see in her!?" Quite simply, that bear of a "Mastiff" is the sweetest most loyal woman he has ever met and makes him feel like he is the best "master" there ever was on earth. She is absolutely beautiful in his eyes, and he loves how she is always steady, devoted, and dutiful. That spindly, nervous "Chihuahua" makes another guy feel like a big protector and giant of a man. When he is by her side and keeping her from shaking in fear, he is king of the world!

What makes a younger woman more attractive than one that is older? What's cuter and more endearing – a nine-week old, romping, droopy-eared, innocent puppy, or the twelve-year old, long-in-the-tooth old gal that doesn't have the pep to get up to go outside? Of course, it's the "puppy," but when the younger qualities of a "puppy" are displayed in a mature woman, the same feelings can be as easily evoked in a man.

Age isn't as big a factor to men as women believe it to be. Many times, the older "pup" who has calmed down, behaves well, is loyal, loving, and doesn't require as much "training" is more desirable to a man than a young "puppy," especially if a man is mature in the real sense of the word and desires compatibility.

Skeptical about The Puppy Principle? However simplistically disappointing and disheartening it might be, there has not been one man to whom I've explained The Puppy Principle who has not wholeheartedly agreed that it is the way he feels about and experiences women. Most importantly, if you can give over to

The Puppy Principle, it will free you to be more understanding of men and their behavior while comprehending what follows: How men commit!

Back to the Breeder

Still on the floor with all the puppies, you've found one that endears you! This one feels so right, and you know he's just perfect. You love the way he comes to you, nuzzles your ear and seems to connect with you when you take his little head in your hands and look into his eyes. While all the others are still running around, this little one has sidled up next to you and sits there sweetly, lightly licking your hand. You're in love. You've found "The One!"

Ms. Breeder comes back in and you excitedly show her your pick to take home. "Oh dear, I'm so sorry," she says. "I forgot to take him out. He's already been adopted."

You're crestfallen. Ms. Breeder takes your special little guy out of your arms and out of the room.

How He Bounces Back So Fast

How long is it before you're back to petting, playing, and fully engaging with the other puppies again? Five minutes? Ten minutes? Likely, it won't be very long until you've forgotten your first pick, as other little precious pups in front of you are drawing your attention and making you feel comforted just by the sights, sounds, and smells of them!

In a short time, if another pup in the group strikes your fancy, you are likely to consider adopting that puppy just as much as the first that you chose. If not, you may leave a bit disappointed, yet you'll do so having enjoyed your time with the little cuties, all with the knowledge that there are plenty of puppies in the world with whom you can easily fall in love. You'll simply go looking again and in no time flat, you'll have a puppy to call your own.

Welcome again to how a man feels when he is merely infatuated. Before he's hopelessly fallen in love and, most importantly, *formally committed*, he has no feelings of being bonded to any one woman. Because he is attracted to *all women* in one way, shape, or form (just as you find all puppies to be cute to one degree or another), a man knows he can easily become infatuated and will always be able to find a "pretty pup" that he will want to take home for one night or a lifetime.

His Focus Is Fleeting

The Puppy Principle also explains what happens when a man seems so connected to you in the moment only to forget all about you the next. It's why he might not remember a date, or to call, text, or follow up with you. The ease with which a man can be distracted by a "puppy" explains a host of issues that women experience with men.

Even after you've made a real connection with a fantastic first date, the next day when he is out and a cute "puppy" crosses his path, he may just "follow her home" and ask her out. With all the cute "puppies" out and about – even if you're in a relationship – some men can still be so easily distracted that they will completely forget that you're waiting at home with the newspaper and slippers!

Part of His Process

You're back on the floor now with Laura when another precious puppy comes up to you. This one crawled up on your chest, licked your nose, and promptly fell asleep. He couldn't be any cuter. You feel his little puppy breath on your neck and you're in love again. You've forgotten all about your first pick of a few minutes ago and when Ms. Breeder comes back in, you share the good news that you're hooked again!

Before leaving to get the adoption papers, Ms. Breeder notices Laura still cuddling a special, shy little girl that she has been holding while the other pups have been jumping up and trying to get her attention. Laura hasn't been able to put this particular puppy down since she first set eyes on her and picked her up.

"It seems like she's really fallen for you," Ms. Breeder says. "I can give you a good deal on her because your friend is adopting today. Why don't you take her home? It looks like she loves you, and that you're starting to fall for her, too!"

Laura gets a sad look on her face. "Oh, my," she sighs. "She is the cutest little girl ever! I just love her, but...."

You immediately stop Laura from continuing and say, "Laura, she is perfect, you've got to take her! Don't risk losing her. You'll regret it if you walk out of here! She might not be here if you change your mind!"

How He Decides

Laura almost tears up as she hands the puppy over to the breeder. "I'm so sorry, but please understand. This little puppy is just the best, most adorable thing ever, and I'm already beginning to fall in love with her. But, I just started a new job, and I just can't give her all the attention she is going to need. I'm still paying off my student loans and don't have the funds available should she need anything or get sick. I also don't know how long I can stay at my apartment before I have to move. I'm just not settled enough, and I may want to leave my job in a few months. I also want to take the summer to travel in Europe. No matter how much I love her, or how much I want a puppy like her in my life, it's simply not the right time for me to take on the responsibility!"

When His Practical Side Wins

In our little story, Laura represents a man who is not ready to commit because of practical factors in his life. We'll explore the state of this man in the next chapter. For now, it is important to know that for men, commitment is a responsibility for which they must be completely prepared. Despite a man's love for you, if he is not ready to take on the responsibility *he views a committed relationship to be*, he will decide that commitment is not right for him. As was the case with Laura saying no to her beautiful little puppy, a man will not usually forego his rational determinations in favor of his feelings of love.

When He Decides to Engage

You sign for your little guy and you and Laura are out the door. Laura drives while you hold your new little partner on your lap. You think of how you prepared for this moment, so you could handle the extra expense. You remember suffering through your last awful job and feeling proud of yourself for saving some of each paycheck over the last few months. You moved to an apartment closer to work, so you would be able to go home at lunch to attend to your new love and take him out. A month ago, you began walking every night to ensure that you developed the habit and would be comfortable taking your new puppy out before you go to bed.

You took the time to discover if you were truly ready to take on the responsibility of another being. Now you can't wait to get to the pet shop to buy your little guy that faux-diamond collar you've been eying. That special sparker states to the world that this is your guy! You are so excited to think of the years ahead and all the love and experiences you will have together.

How He Convinces Himself

While on the drive, your new puppy starts to fuss and then vomits on your lap. Laura looks at you skeptically and asks, "Are you sure this is something you really want to commit to?" You cheerfully reach for the towel you brought with you and exclaim with glee, "I do!"

You both laugh, as Laura confides that she is "so relieved" that she didn't give in to temptation and adopt the puppy she fell in love with. "I am so not ready to take on that kind of responsibility," she says. She continues on to say out loud what convinced her to overcome her feelings and stick to her decision.

"I'm so glad I was able to resist the beautiful eyes on that puppy," she sighs. "I'll be more set financially next year when I'm finished paying off my loans and credit cards. I also want to trek through Europe this summer before I look for a new job. I'll definitely adopt someday, but now is not the right time. I know she'll find a good home that is better than I could provide at the moment, that's for sure! She'd be alone a lot, and she deserves to have someone who is around more. I still have so many other things I want to be doing. There'll be another puppy I'll love just as much...when I'm really ready!"

You congratulate Laura on making a sound decision as you hold your puppy close and begin to bond with him. Laura reaches over and pets him often during the drive home as she promises you that she'll be there to take him on weekends and when you need to go visit your parents. You just can't wait to get home to settle in with your new love. Each passing moment with him reinforces your decision that he is "the one" for you.

It's the Principle

The Puppy Principle provides you with a way to understand how you are viewed and loved by men. It also provides you with insight into how men view commitment and why love and desire are not enough for a man to commit. With these key concepts, you are now ready to learn about the two states that men live in. One state allows a man to take on the responsibility of commitment and the other state does not. Once you are able to recognize which state a man is in, you will be able to make informed choices about the men you date or the man with whom you are currently involved, so you can move your love life forward.

Chapter Four
Is He Just Consuming You?

I n Chapter 3, you likely recognized Laura to be in a
state of flux in her life and not ready to take on the
responsibility of pet ownership. Despite her great love
of puppies and a strong desire to have a doggie in her life,
she was not prepared to purchase or adopt, and she wouldn't
allow herself to be pressured into it. Laura wasn't ready, willing,
or able to make the commitment she knew was necessary to be
a responsible pet owner, especially as that relates to financial
strain and restriction of her freedom. Laura knows she will one
day be ready, but until that time, she is unwilling to sacrifice
her free time, money, and liberty in exchange for the love of a
canine companion.

Like it or not, this is how a man can feel about a formal romantic commitment, most specifically, marriage because marriage has an inherently formal and legal/financial component

of responsibility that a man takes very seriously. In our story, you represent a man being ready, willing, and able to commit. Because you prepared and felt ready and able to take on the responsibility of a puppy, you went out and got one – it was that simple. In some ways, when the time is right for a man to be in a committed relationship, it is that simple for him to go out and pick a cute "puppy!"

Once a man has his educational, financial, and professional life in order and has fulfilled all the single-life experiences he feels he wants to have had before "settling down," he will commit. This fact is borne out by statistics, as well as what we see socially. According to the US Census of 2012, only 20% of adults aged twenty-five and up have never been married. That means a whopping 80% of adults are married or have been married, at least once. Men want to commit and do commit, they just have to be in the right state of being to do so! They have to be in a state of readiness, willingness, and ability to take on a responsibility for the long run. They have to be in the state of a being a Buyer.

The Consumer State

In our hypothetical trip to the breeder, Laura illustrated a man when he is in a state of being a Consumer. Just because Laura wasn't ready to take on the responsibility of a puppy doesn't mean that she doesn't love puppies. Laura actually loves puppies more than most things in life, and she dreams about having her own puppy one day.

Laura is, with puppies, the way most men are with women. Just like Laura spends several hours a day online, viewing and sharing everyone's cute puppy photos, a busy man finds the time to view lots of women's profiles online. Just as Laura volunteers a few times a week at a shelter just to be around puppies, and she regularly donates money to a national charity for pets, a man spends money looking for women and dating. Just as when Laura wants to relax after a stressful day, she'll sometimes go to the dog park just to watch the dogs run and play together, a man casually sleeps with women and may spend part of his free time looking at women on erotic websites.

Laura's interest and time spent on her love of puppies does not mean she is ready, willing or able to take one home. When a man is a Consumer, he is like Laura. He "consumes" a woman or lots of women, but he won't commit.

Consumers are simply men who love "puppies" in all shapes, sizes, colors and ages. "Puppies" are all cute, comforting, and crazy-making to men – the good kind of crazy-making! A man will consume any amount of time, attention, and affection a cute "puppy" will give him, for as long as she is willing and makes it easy for him. If he's in a state of being a Consumer, the man will not "adopt." This is true whether or not the man is in love with a particular "pup."

A Man Is in the State of Being a Consumer When He:

- Has not achieved his educational, career or avocational goals and believes he will not be able to achieve them while in a relationship.

- Has not fulfilled the single-life experiences he wants to have had before settling down with one woman.

- Lacks confidence he can be faithful.

- Is not financially successful/stable or feeling capable of becoming so, while in a relationship.

- Is, or is not, in love.

It's important to note that being in love will <u>not</u> usually trump any of the first four items on the List of Consumer Characteristics. A man is not a Buyer simply because he is in love. Remember, he's a man – a being who can love all women to one degree or another.

When a man is a Consumer, he will consume a woman he likes (or even loves) for as long as she is willing to be consumed with no intention of making a commitment. With rare exception, a Consumer will leave a woman he loves, rather than take on the responsibility of a relationship before he has fulfilled the first four items on the list of Consumer Characteristics.

Don't Be Taken for a Ride

In the world of car sales, the slang for consumers is "tire-kickers." Tire-kickers are guys (usually) who just love to go to the new car lots, look at all the shiny new models, take in their sights and smells, talk to the salesman about all the latest features, take test drives, and generally walk around kicking tires. Tire-kickers have no real intention of signing on a dotted line and buying a new car. No matter how good the sales pitch, a tire kicker is very unlikely to buy. This doesn't mean that it never happens, it's simply rare. For a deal to be sealed, it takes a great deal of patience, determination, and haggling on the part of the salesperson.

Prospective Buyers walk on to a new car lot truly in the market to purchase a car. They've done their research, selected their particular model, and either gotten their finances together, or know how the financing works. The salesperson needs to do very little to sell to a Buyer. The transaction with a buyer happens easily, naturally, and within a reasonable amount of time.

Consumers are the relationship equivalent of tire-kickers. While Consumers love to take in the wonderful sights, smells and features of the latest "models" – taking them out for long "test drives" – they generally waste the time and effort of the well-intentioned saleswoman looking to seal a deal.

Put Him to The Test

Many women want to know if there is anything that can be done to transition a Consumer to a Buyer. Just as with the salesperson trying get a tire-kicker to make a deal, it can take a great deal of time and effort with little to no guarantee of success. It is a serious gambling game. While the game certainly depends on the category of Consumer into which a man falls, and other factors unique to each relationship, it mostly depends on the steps a woman is willing to take, her emotional resolve to take the steps, and her level of patience once the steps are taken. Time, by itself, will not change a Consumer into a Buyer. This is why it is so important to scale a man on where he is *at this moment*. You can do this by taking the Consumer vs. Buyer Relationship Test – a test I created to identify a man's state of readiness, willingness, and ability to commit.

I make the Consumer vs. Buyer Relationship Test available to any woman reading this book simply by logging on to my website. By completing the test, you will know where any man with whom you're involved falls on the Consumer vs Buyer scale. To complete the test and view the results, go to www.coachpaulagrooms.com.

No Judgments

The Consumer vs. Buyer Relationship concept is not about categorizing men as good or bad, right or wrong. Most Consumers do not purposely set out to disappoint, hoodwink, or otherwise hurt women. Does the tire-kicker step onto the car lot with complete awareness that he is not going to buy? Sometimes yes and sometimes no. Mostly, the tire-kicker is so infatuated with the new models that he can't help himself from wanting to take in all their gloriousness and go for test drives. Sometimes he knowingly wastes the time of the salesperson and others he fools himself into believing that he "just might buy" if the car is right. There are times when he just wants to try-out a different make or model. There are other times when he just can't help himself from stopping by the dealer to check out a sale. Make no mistake though. If a guy doesn't have his finances in order to buy the model that he wants and that he can comfortably afford, he will walk out of the dealership having wasted the time of the salesperson, justifying and telling himself that it was the "poor salesmanship," "the wrong deal," or in some way "just wasn't the right time."

When He's Not in The Market

In the next few chapters, you'll learn a great deal more about the two types of Consumers and two types of Buyers. You'll also get to know the 8 Toxic Consumers to avoid. For now, I want you to fully understand a man's state of being as a Consumer and for that, I need to ask you a favor.

Will You Take Him to Be Yours?

I have a puppy, and I need your help. I have to spend every weekend with my sick grandmother who lives where pets are strictly forbidden. You love dogs, so I ask you to please take my little guy, Scout, every Friday night until I come back on Monday to pick him up.

Scout is a great dog – the kind you take home to mother! Easy to be with, comes when called, walks off-leash, and is a guy magnet! You love being with Scout. Each Friday, you look forward to having him with you for the weekend. You take him to sidewalk cafes to have dinner and brunch. You tie him up outside when you visit your local shops, and everyone in your neighborhood is getting to know him and love him. A few of the store's owners have given you treats for Scout, and you enjoy the comments about how he is "so cute and well-behaved." All your friends are fond of him and tell you how adorable you are together. They always remind you what a great dog he is and tell you that you aren't likely to ever find a better-behaved pup.

Because he loves it so much, you enjoy giving Scout a bath in your tub, even though it makes a mess. He looks so cute when he's all lathered up, and you love how excited he gets after he is dried off and starts shaking the towel and prancing around your apartment like he owns the place. You take lots of selfies together, and he sleeps with you in bed every night.

It's so comforting and relaxing to have Scout share your weekends. On several occasions, you've been sick, and just having Scout there to keep you company made you feel better. You were just coming off a terrible breakup when you decided to take Scout, and it made you feel instantly better to have him around. You've grown to really love the little guy! You don't mind spending almost anything on him when he's with you – so much so that you find you can't pass a pet store without getting a little something he'll like.

Some weekends, you take Scout to your friend's beach house or to visit your parents. Your father adores him, and you love watching the two of them play fetch in the yard. Your dad gets up each morning you're there and takes Scout for long walks. He's told you that Scout makes him feel younger! While you sense your mom worries that Scout is causing your dad to think about getting his own puppy, you see that she really loves having Scout come home with you, and having him with you makes the weekends a bit more special.

Every Monday when I come to retrieve Scout, you are sad for a moment. As I gather up his toys and treats to leave, you keep kissing and hugging him, and telling him, "I love you, Scout!" as we head out the door. He stops midway in the hall to look back at you, signaling that he feels close to you too, and that he knows he belongs with you in some way. It tugs at your heart, but when you shut the door and start your week, you don't think much about Scout again until I arrive with him the next Friday night.

Our arrangement goes on for ten months. When I remind you how long it's been, you're shocked, as you really didn't think much about it. The time merely passed. You always knew you'd take care of Scout for me as long it worked for you, and you wanted to keep doing it.

Calling Him Out on His Consumerism

"We need to talk," I say one Monday when I come to your door. "I now have to take care of my grandmother permanently and need to move in with her." I look at you very seriously and grab your hand. "I know you love Scout, so I'm giving him to you to be totally yours."

You are completely taken aback. How could I think that you would want Scout to be yours full-time? The room starts spinning. As you catch your breath, you begin to tell me why it is that you can't take this dog. You have a list of all the things you are looking to do in the next few years, including taking that promotion you know you'll be offered in the next few months. You want to start training for the marathon, saving for a house, and taking an African safari. Besides, although you love Scout, the weekend arrangement wasn't permanent!

You tell me you thought you were just hanging out with Scout without any strings attached and that's what made it so great for you. You felt free, and it was fun to have Scout like he was yours – minus the responsibility. To take Scout full-time was not what you signed up for. When you look down at him patiently watching us talk, wagging his tail and lovingly gazing up at you, he now doesn't look so cute. He's making you feel guilty. This isn't at all what you wanted!

I'm shocked and can't believe you wouldn't want to be with Scout forever. "I don't understand," I say. "You've shared a great relationship with him for ten whole months! You've been going out together to dinners and brunch, shopping and the park –

you've even introduced him to your parents, who happen to love him! Everyone has seen you together for nearly a year now, and your friends all tell you he's "great!"

I keep going on and on about it being "unfair" to Scout and remind you of all the good things you've ever said about him. "Scout's been there with you in good times and bad," I point out. "You've had tons of fun, and you yourself have said he couldn't be any cuter or easier to be with. What more could you want?"

I continue to admonish you and become more and more upset at your lack of showing emotion. "For goodness sake," I say in disbelief. "You've been sleeping together every weekend for nearly a year! How could you? You told me you love him! How can you not want him as yours forever!?"

You Are a Consumer Too

Women have all had experiences as Consumers, yet we blast men who live in the state of being unable to commit because they are not ready to take on what they see as a responsibility. Because women view commitment as a natural outgrowth of love, it is sometimes challenging to step into the shoes of a Consumer. In our hypothetical tale involving Scout, being tied down with a pet would restrict your current and foreseeable future freedom. The driving motivation behind your Consumerism involved being mature and true to your own needs despite how much you loved Scout.

The shock you felt when I asked you to adopt Scout permanently is what a Consumer feels when faced with a woman making assumptions. Women often assume that time spent together, expressed feelings, and a desire for fun, friendship, sleeping together, and the experience of being part of a couple automatically means a man wants to be in a committed relationship for the long-term.

When a man is in the state of being a Consumer, he'll embrace it when you're there for him in the bad times and when he isn't feeling well. He'll relish every moment of taking you on walks, hanging out, having meals, taking bubble baths, sleeping together, frolicking in your apartment, going on trips, and even introducing you to his family and friends. Though he does not want the responsibility of a long-term relationship, this doesn't make him a bad person. Having other things that he wants to take care of before committing to be responsible to a wife and the possible children that can come from a union doesn't make him a bad man. He takes your continuing to hang out on the weekends as acceptance of things as they are. He figures your "bark" (what you say to him) doesn't mean much because you don't "bite" (show him, through behavior, that you don't accept his unwillingness to commit).

Chapter Five
His State of Affairs

The state of being either a Consumer or a Buyer is individualized for each man. A man lives in one state or another according to having fulfilled his deepest needs of achievement, independence, and connection to other people. When in the state of a Consumer, a man will not commit because he does not feel ready and capable of taking on the responsibility of a wife and/or children. Modern women balk at this premise because they know that they are capable of taking care of themselves and, in most cases, do not require a man to support them or even their children. While this is rational and may be factual, it doesn't change a man's reasoning, feelings, or state of being.

No matter how far we have come sociologically and technologically, a man's biological and anthropological drives are to hunt, procreate by spreading his seed, and provide for and protect his family clan. Women's inherent biological and anthropological drives are to procreate and nurture offspring to adulthood. These distinctive drives are for the purpose of humans surviving as a species. While primal drives may look different in today's world, our deepest hard-wiring is as the mammal beings that we are.

Men still receive deep ego-gratifying satisfaction from providing, protecting, procreating, and proving they can attain what it is they aim to achieve. Now, instead of bringing home a kill to feed his clan, a modern man "hunts and fights" in whatever career he has chosen. In present day, a guy proves his manhood by succeeding in the world so that he can afford the best food and maintain the safest and best "cave" for his family.

No longer does a man have to be physically stronger than other men to become "king of the jungle." In modern society, intellectual, athletic, or artistic achievement, as well as attaining the most desirable woman or women and other material goods, provide men with a sense of accomplishment. Achievements serve to display a man's success to the world, especially to other men or competitors.

No matter which time period we're talking about, a man's ability to provide for his family and/or to be the "top lion of the pride" (his circle of peers) is the way in which he identifies and judges himself as a success or failure.

A man also forms and maintains his sense of identity by knowing, feeling, and being seen as a strong, competent, achieved, and knowledgeable creator, builder, and "fixer" of tangible things, not emotional needs. These identity needs are as intrinsic to men as most women's inherent needs are to feel desired, loved, and honored by those to whom they feel connected.

Generally, a woman's needs are not as "fixed" as a man's. Whether this is due to the greater inter-hemispheric exchange in a woman's brain or a greater flexibility in societal norms is open to debate. Though it appears to be a bit of both, the scientific/medical community is beginning to see the greater influence of nature versus nurture.

Boys to Men

As boys grow into men, they generally spend most of their time and energy to prove their male prowess to the world intellectually, athletically, financially, or in some way related to achievement. Want to test this notion? See how a man reacts to not knowing something or being able to do something that he deems as inherently masculine. Conversely, observe how uncomfortable a man becomes when forced to do something that he views as inherently feminine. Again, this will be to a greater or lesser degree depending on where a man falls on the horizontal line of gender traits, but generally speaking, men do not spend a great deal of their time thinking about their relationships. Men focus on achieving tangible goals. When interested in a particular woman, a man's goal can include proving that he is her pick over an equally adept challenger, even if he wasn't particularly interested in the woman when the challenger was not present.

Time is No Present

Men have a difficult time understanding why it is that women think so much about the future of their romantic relationships because they believe that committed relationships simply happen "when it's the right time." Men are innately attracted to most all females and anthropologically wired to spread their seed at any given time. This vast difference from women affords men the knowledge that when the time is perfect, they can easily find a woman to whom they will be attracted, and it is then that they will take on the responsibility of commitment.

Men do not think about or relate to time through their relationships. Men mostly relate to time in terms of their education, career goals, and avocational interests. Ask a man when he plans to graduate, what he has planned for his entire career until he retires, or how he is training for an upcoming triathlon, and he'll lay out an intricate mental map complete with verbal graphs and timeline charts. He may even have everything planned and plotted out on an app. Ask him about his plans for marriage and having a family, and he'll likely say something vague like "someday" or "before I'm too old to play catch with my kids."

A man is mainly focused *on the moment* and is *in the moment* in terms of his relationships. If it feels good and is without complication *now*, then that's all that matters to him. A man will decide "tomorrow" if his relationship supports, or at least doesn't get in the way of, his main reason-to-be: to achieve and prove himself to be strong, capable, and competent in whatever he is doing professionally, educationally, artistically, athletically, or anything else in which he endeavors.

A Man's Time Warp

Many women make the mistake of interpreting a man's state of being ready "when it's the right time" to mean when a man *feels* enough for a woman to commit to her. Beware of falling into this trap. Again, while neither is right or wrong, men do not plan their lives based on their feelings. They direct their lives through decisions that will make them feel and appear competent and accomplished.

He Is His Decisions

Part of being seen as accomplished is being in control of one's life and environment. A man's feelings will almost always take a backseat to his idea of what will allow him to be viewed as a man who is in control of his life – and sometimes in control of the people in his life. This is due to the fact that some men view their choice of partner (and the children resulting from that choice) as directly reflecting on their *ability to make good decisions*. Depending on the man, he may work hard to maintain control of his spouse and children so that neither reflects negatively on whether he is viewed by others as competent.

Separate the Man from His State

Even if your man has not made the final decision to commit to you, he could still be an absolutely wonderful guy who really loves you. But without making a decision to commit, he is merely enjoying whatever time, attention, and affection you care to give him *in the moment*. He may listen to your laments about not locking things down and depending upon his level of caring for you, he may even make attempts to satisfy your desires or take a stab at "trying." He likely loves you in many ways and certainly loves being with you – if not, he would have left. Remember Scout? While you loved spending the weekends with my wonderful pup, you didn't want to take him on as a full time and lifetime responsibility. Thus, no matter a man's love or desire, if he is in the state of being a Consumer, his feelings will not override his decisions. The number one Core Principle of my Cognitive Commitment Component of Men explains how men and women view commitment very differently.

Women View Commitment as a Natural Outgrowth of Love; Men View Commitment as a Responsibility.

As you have learned by reading this book, the divergent view of commitment causes women to misinterpret the actions and intentions of men. This is easily done, as the actions of Consumers can be exactly the same as the actions of Buyers, especially in the beginning of any relationship.

Consumers Are A Given; Buyers Prove Themselves

Initially, any man who is interested in you will appear to be a Buyer. This is typically not by design or to mislead you and is the case whether a man's interest is purely sexual or has the potential to be more. As a man, he can't help but do what comes naturally to him, which is to pursue females! If you're really attracted to a man, you will tend to view his actions through the lens of your own desire and believe that he is pursuing you as a Buyer. It is critical to remember that a man's pursuit will be to the degree that he is willing to put in the work for the possibility of having sex with you. Nothing less and *nothing more*! This isn't bad or wrong; it's simply male.

To avoid disappointment and hurt, keep yourself from interpreting a man's initial interest (no matter how intense) as anything more than sexual. That interest will show itself in many ways that can lead you to believe that a relationship is on his mind. Until he says that it is, it isn't, and his words must be consistent with his actions. As I remind my clients: "When in doubt, wait him out!" Waiting is the *first* step in separating Consumers from Buyers.

In Dating and Relationships: Think Marathon, Not Sprint!

The Rules, the dating "bible" that made every best-seller list in the United States when it was released in 1995, remains the guide for every woman who wants to have a divinely committed relationship with a man who cherishes her. It outlines the way a woman needs to behave, interact, and conduct herself for the greatest possibility of success with any man from the very first interaction, up to and including every year of marriage. Following The Rules is a way to ensure the greatest possibility of success. Doing The Rules weeds out Consumers and only leaves the most committed Buyers in a woman's life.

When a man is a Buyer, he will comply with The Rules, and you will know his interest is more than just sexual. If he is a Buyer, he will honor and respect your needs because he will want you for more than sex.

> **Men who want you just for sex will push and pout.**
>
> **Men who want you for more than sex will show respect and restraint.**

While waiting to have sex can be equally difficult for both you and him, it's important to wait, not merely because it will reveal a man's true state of being and separate Consumers from Buyers, but because if a man has the ability to wait (and wonder), he will fall in love! This is the best gift you, as a woman, can give to a man. This is because of the way a man loves. The way in which men fall in love and most importantly, stay in love, is vital to understand in order to be successful in your romantic relationships.

Men Love Through Wondering and Longing.

The Rules, by Ellen Fein and Sherrie Schneider, as well as their follow-up books such as *Not Your Mother's Rules* and *The Rules for Marriage*, give women the best chance of success with men. Whether just starting out, or married for decades, the approaches and strategies of The Rules allow for men to love in the deepest possible male way of loving – through *wondering*! Additionally, when a woman fosters a Rules relationship with a man, she is affording herself the deepest possible female way of loving – through *knowing*. When a man has accepted a woman's practice of The Rules, the woman knows, without any doubt, that she is loved, valued, and cherished.

Wonder of Wonders, Miracle of Miracles

It is easy to make men wonder in both big and small ways. Many times, the wonder is as simple as a man thinking and asking himself questions such as:

- Why hasn't she texted back yet?
- Will she answer my call?
- Where is she now?
- Will tonight be the night we have sex?
- Does she think I'm great at (fill in the blank)?

At other times, the wonder can be more profound, as in:

- Am I the guy she wants over every other guy?
- Do I turn her on enough so that she won't want another man?
- Does she think I'm worthy to be with her?
- Am I achieved enough to keep her in the lifestyle I see her as being worthy of?

No matter the degree, this *wonder* needs to be maintained consistently in order for a man to remain in love. A man needs to keep wondering, proving, guessing, longing, and trying to achieve a woman's time, attention and affection. This allows a man to love as men do. In turn, this allows you to love as you do, and are happiest doing: through *knowing* a man's love and devotion is real and true.

Chapter Six
The Consumers – The Good, the Bad, and the Ugly

Have you ever wondered why it is that a man distanced himself or left you when you absolutely knew with 100% certainty that he loved you, desired you, and wanted to be with you? Were you devastated and confused, while he seemed cold and completely unwilling to give over to his emotions? If this has happened to you, you experienced a breakup with a Consumer: a man who is not ready to be in a committed relationship, no matter his feelings.

A man will not share his feelings at the expense of what he values most: adherence to his decisions. Living by decisions accomplishes two important goals: separating "the men from the boys" and highlighting the differences between men and women. The Cognitive Commitment Component of Men explains this male phenomenon.

Men Do Not Act *from* Their Feelings or Act *on* Their Feelings.

Men Make Decisions About What They Think Is Right for Them and Those They Love and Care About *Regardless* of Their Feelings.

You may be thinking that a man is acting on his feelings when he is with you as a Consumer – and you would be right! A Consumer is acting on his feelings of wanting to be with you, and because you accept his lack of commitment, he is *making a decision* that you are okay with the way things are. He is deciding that things are right for him and right for you, *right now*!

A woman who no longer accepts the consumeristic state forces the Consumer to make a decision about committing. It is only when a woman forces the issue of commitment that a man will make a decision about what is right for him and – if he is a good guy – right for you, regardless of his feelings.

If a man respects you, and if he loves or cares for you personally, he will distance himself and not look back until he is ready, willing, and able to make a commitment to you. This could be in a month or in a decade. In some cases, it could be in many years, long after you've moved on and only after he has sown many wild oats. He may then look for you because he remembers how he *felt* and now feels ready to give you what he always knew you deserved.

Depending on the man, if you make the choice to remove yourself from a relationship with a Consumer, at times his feelings will overwhelm him, and he may flip-flop. At these times, if you're not strong in your resolve to gain a commitment, your relationship will be unclear, undefined, and stuck in a negative and time-wasting pattern. This is due to a very important rule of thumb of a Consumer vs. Buyer Relationship:

No Amount of Time, by Itself, Turns a Consumer into a Buyer.

Playing His Cards

Once a man is called out on his unwillingness to commit and his hand is forced on the issue, he will act, meaning he will enact the Cognitive Commitment Component; however, his enacting it now does not mean that it wasn't there all along. Not being ready, willing, or able to commit is always present for a man when he is in the state of being a Consumer. Women don't recognize or accept this fact because they live by their feelings.

Until such time as you insist on a commitment in order to continue in a relationship, a Consumer will blissfully live without a thought of changing anything. Once you make it known that you are unhappy with a man's consumeristic state, you change the unspoken contract between the two of you and force his hand. The Consumer vs. Buyer Relationship Test determines whether or not that hand will be for marriage or on the doorknob for the nearest exit.

I developed the Consumer vs. Buyer Relationship Test to help you assess the viability of any relationship. At any time while reading this book, you can connect to me at www.coachpaulagrooms.com for free access to the test and the results.

The Consumer vs. Buyer Relationship Test and Scores

Regardless of whether you are currently in a relationship, you'll likely recognize one or all of the different types of Consumers.

The Ultimate Consumer (3 – 28 Score)

The lowest scoring Consumer is The Ultimate Consumer. Scoring in this range indicates a man's current inability and/or lack of desire to be in a relationship beyond the purely sexual.

The Mixed-Messages Consumer (29 – 59 Score)

The Mixed-Message Consumer exhibits the behaviors of a man who fluctuates between wanting some kind of convenient relationship while being pulled by his own needs on the List of Consumer Characteristics. Simply put, this man is a vacillator. At certain times, he shows himself to be a full-fledged Ultimate

Consumer. At others, he reaches the point of straddling the line of the next category: The Prospective Buyer.

The Prospective Buyer (60 – 90 Score)

The Prospective Buyer has checked off most items on the List of Consumer Characteristics and is in love with the woman with whom he is involved. Whatever his score, however, The Prospective Buyer still has questions or concerns that he hasn't answered or resolved. These concerns can either be related to the woman he is with or not.

The Bona Fide Buyer (91 – 106 Score)

The Bona Fide Buyer has decided to commit and is totally in love. While there is still room for this man to renege on his decision – as he is not bonded until he has made a formal commitment that he makes public – he is the most likely of The Buyers to take his decision to the ultimate level of commitment.

Obviously, the lower the score in any category, the less committed a man is, and the higher the score, the more a man leans towards commitment. Regardless, anything less than a declaration of a man's feelings and direct expression of his desire to commit indicates a possible lack of intention and/or definitive decision on his part. Without desire, there is no possibility of a decision. Without a decision, there is no possibility of a commitment. Without a formal commitment, there is no possibility that a man will bond.

Go to www.coachpaulagrooms.com and connect with me to take the test and get your score. Read on to understand your results.

The Ultimate Consumer (3 – 28 Score)

The word Ultimate starts with a U and so does the word unfortunately. On the scale of Consumer vs. Buyer, should you want more than a fleeting affair, this is an unfortunate category for your man to fall. The Ultimate Consumer offers the lowest possibility of a real relationship. It doesn't matter if this is his natural state or a lack of feelings for you, but it is definitely one or the other or both.

Whether you've been dating for two weeks or two years, the lower the score, the less likely it is that The Ultimate Consumer is interested in, or capable of, a relationship with you for more than whatever the two of you currently share. This doesn't mean an Ultimate Consumer is a bad guy or even that he doesn't love or care for you on some level. A score in this range could simply mean that a man is not at all where he wants to be in his life in order to take on the responsibility of a relationship.

Unfortunately, you may never know whether The Ultimate Consumer's lack of wanting a commitment is due to the first four items on the List of Consumer Characteristics or his lack of feelings for you. The Ultimate Consumer will not provide any detailed emotional discussions about your relationship. Regardless of your level of feelings, he may not even consider the two of you to be in a relationship. He knows he is disappointing you, and it makes him very uncomfortable to have to face you or discuss the truth of his state of being.

If your man has scored in this range, know that he enjoys what you give him and likes spending whatever time he decides to give you, but he is not considering anything beyond the here and now. While you may be thinking you have some kind of chance, he likely feels you're "nothing serious," or that you're just a "go-to" woman. This Consumer likely doesn't think much about you factoring into his life or consider much of anything beyond what you have together, *at this moment*. He plans nothing beyond what is immediately in front of him. Ultimately, the most this Consumer is comfortable planning with you is for the next few hours. While this can be extremely disappointing, you must accept the reality of this man's score and take action to save yourself from further disappointment or heartbreak. Remember, no amount of time factors into any man's state of being.

Don't let yourself believe that if you've been with a man for a certain length of time, despite his score, he will change his state. If you don't make major changes *now,* you risk a real hit to your self-esteem and will also thwart any chance of this Ultimate Consumer being interested in more with you later – if and when he changes, or he makes major changes to his life.

Think again if you're thinking, "Great, he'll be ready one day!" Know that "one day" may be a very long time in coming if ever. Staying with The Ultimate Consumer does not change him into a Buyer. The *longer* you stay with The Ultimate Consumer, the *greater* the chances that if and when he is ready, willing, and capable of a real relationship, you will not be his "pick of the litter" to "adopt" and take home. While it's a harsh reality, in many cases the man naturally feels he has already "played" with you. Chances are, he'll be looking for a new "puppy" when he is ready to settle down.

Why This Is Ultimately Happening

Ultimate Consumers can be quite attractive and even irresistible! They can be bad boys and challenging on every level which can be very compelling. The Ultimate Consumer can be intoxicating, hypnotic, and extremely charming when with you. It can be downright addictive to not know whether tonight is your last night of bliss in his arms, or if he is going to fulfill your dreams by doing or saying the smallest thing to indicate that he is starting to feel something deeper for you.

Whatever the reasons you have for still dating or seeing this man, continuing to meet the needs of The Ultimate Consumer is a recipe for heartbreak. If you have even the slightest feeling that you might be falling in love and actually entertaining any thoughts of a real relationship with this man now or in the future, your approach and way of interacting with him are of significance in determining a good outcome and of having any chance later on, should you want it.

While nothing will change The Ultimate Consumer's timeline, your guy may have landed in this category because of the way you initially became involved, presented yourself, or pursued him. Without specific strategies to change the dynamic between you, you run the risk of damaging any future chances with this man who, due to what you've *shown him* you will accept, has likely placed you in a category that is less than favorable for any type of serious relationship.

Words Have No Meaning

In Chapter 8, we'll explore how men relate more through actions than words. Suffice it to say, to The Ultimate Consumer, your words fall on deaf ears, and he will almost always relate most to what you *do*, not to what you *say*. He is the ultimate believer, practitioner, and example of the old adage, "actions speak louder than words." In his mind, no matter what you *say*, if you keep seeing him and/or sleeping with him, then to him, you're okay with your relationship exactly the way that it is. The Ultimate Consumer understands that if you are *staying* – no matter what you are *saying* – you are good with the status quo.

If at any time he becomes dissatisfied "hanging out" with you, an Ultimate Consumer will simply walk away without any fanfare or in extreme cases, not even so much as a text. Because he operates at this level, he thinks you do as well. Any attempts at discussing your feelings or his actions will be met with defensiveness, anger, or him shutting down completely. Whether this is because you didn't inspire more in him or because this is his baseline consumeristic level, the odds of any real relationship materializing with an Ultimate Consumer are rarely good.

Accepting the Status Quo

If you choose to continue with "Mr. Ultimate," it's important that you be very honest with yourself about what you ultimately want. Are you trying to show yourself to be such a cool and desirable woman that he couldn't possibly not want to be with you? It is important to ask yourself if you really want to be with him, or if you just want to be wanted by him?

If the answer is that you really want this man and feel you can't move forward in life without him, however remote, there are things you can do to see if there is any possibility for this relationship. Seeing the reality of your situation is the only place to start. From there, I offer approaches and strategies with my clients to give them an effective way of seeing if The Ultimate Consumer they love and desire is capable of moving up the scale.

It's a big commitment to execute the strategies necessary to reset and restart your relationship with an Ultimate Consumer. In order to have any chance of inspiring his desire for more, it takes a great deal of effort, patience, and a lot of time apart. Timing is everything when it comes to challenging The Ultimate Consumer's lack of commitment. If you are in such a place, getting support and guidance is going to make the difference in terms of success in the relationship and also for you personally.

The Mixed-Messages Consumer (29 – 59 Score)

On the Consumer vs. Buyer Relationship Scale, The Mixed-Messages Consumer scores between The Ultimate Consumer and The Prospective Buyer. This Consumer is harder to give up than The Ultimate Consumer because this man shows a modicum of desire to fulfill some of your needs at least some of the time. Most of the time though, you may not know where you stand, how he really feels, or if he even considers the two of you to be in a relationship. One day, you have his full attention, devotion, and time and the next, you feel like you don't exist.

Being with a Mixed-Messages Consumer can be difficult and frustrating because he is just good enough to keep you hooked. The good times, while intermittent and mostly on his terms and schedule, can be so great that it's hard to bring yourself to stop seeing him. He may tell you he isn't ready for anything committed or serious, but then acts like the best boyfriend ever and may even declare his love.

A Mixed-Messages Consumer can wreak havoc on your heart and soul. One moment you feel strong and completely capable of riding the roller coaster he has you on, and the next you are standing in a puddle of tears, feeling as emotionally out-of-control as a two-year-old who has lost her favorite stuffed animal. You feel good when receiving the attention and care of Mr. Mixed, but you feel like tearing your hair out when he acts as if you're hardly an item or when he goes totally off the grid.

Despite his occasional declarations of caring or devotion, this knight has no shining armor and requires you to put in most of the work for this relationship to avoid complete distress. Depending on the dynamic between you, you will be faced with having to either leave, pull back a great deal, or you may have to start being more vulnerable, open, and easy. The dynamics of a relationship with The Mixed-Message Consumer can, at times, be reciprocal in nature, and his actions may be directly proportionate to yours. It is important to discover if your attitude, actions, or words have been contributing to his inability to trust that he can be himself with you. If this is not the case, he may simply be your garden-variety Mixed-Messages man.

Mixing It Up

Success with a Mixed-Messages Consumer lies in discovering what is going on between you and your own motives related to this man and to love relationships in general. In order to manifest change, you need to start with yourself and figure out the signals you are giving out. It is likely that your messages to him are as mixed as the ones you are receiving. One way to test this is for you to simply stop doing all that you are doing. Simply stop.

Stop all the texting, calling, emailing, and seeing him on the spur of the moment. No need to give any explanation – just stop. By stopping what you are doing, you are changing the dynamic and reciprocal nature of your relationship. This allows you to see what your Mr. Mixed is willing to do, wants to do, and what he will follow through with. This small change on your part may turn this "mix" into more of a solid entity. Much more will be needed, but this simple test is a good place to begin.

He Knows

Whether you've stated your true feelings or not, most men know that you want more and by not acting on your own needs, you lower his level of respect for you and interest in you. You may think you're hiding your real feelings and that he believes what you've told him about being "okay with how things are." Remember, *men relate through actions and not words.* A Consumer only understands one thing: if you're with him, you accept his behavior and the contract of your relationship as it is, not what you want it to be or *say* you want it to be.

Despite a low score, there is a modicum of hope with The Mixed-Messages Consumer. To have any chance of something meaningful or long-term with this man now or in the future, it's going to take a great deal of emotional self-control and commitment to rectify what was likely a very mixed-messages start when you first met. But don't despair; there is hope if you can change the dynamic and unspoken contract between you.

Institute the stopping technique mentioned above, and not just for a day. Make it a permanent part of your interaction with this man. You are going to have to stop sending your own mixed messages and become firm in your resolve to either run this very long marathon with no end ribbon in sight or move on.

Toxic Consumers

One of the most precious of a woman's commodities is her time. When a woman gives of her time, she gives her attention, and most of the time her attention leads to her connecting, caring, loving, and nurturing. If a woman likes a man, chooses to spend time with him, and then has satisfying sex with him, she is quite likely to fall in love. It is then that she becomes bonded. Bonding to a Toxic Consumer is just like what it sounds – harmful and noxious! It's crazy-making glue!

While all Consumers are typically time wasters, there are 8 particularly Toxic Consumers who will not only strip you of your time, but can potentially play with your head as well. While all Consumers have a low probability of becoming Buyers in the foreseeable future, or are simply not going to be Buyers for you specifically, the following list of Consumers are considered toxic because of their extremely low probability of *ever* becoming Buyers.

1: The Man as a Best Friend

There are men, gay or straight, that truly become a woman's best friend. Depending on the particulars of both your life and his, this friend could be a Consumer. While the most benign of all of the Toxic Consumers, this man is still consuming your valuable time and likely keeping available and interested men at bay.

If your best friend is gay, you may be thinking it's absolutely harmless to spend your weekends together until such time as you find a romantic partner. While you want to spend time with your friend, it's the degree of time and emotional investment that is of importance in the context of your dating life and finding a love relationship. The social and relational needs being met from this friendship can keep you from pursuing interests or activities where you may meet appropriate and available men to date.

If you make your gay male friend a top priority socially, you run the risk of having your romantic needs take a back seat and perhaps shut down completely.

Let's say you and your gay male best friend enjoy going out together. Contrary to popular belief, men who might go up to you if you're out alone won't feel comfortable approaching you if you are with a man, gay or straight. While you may believe that it is obvious that you are with a gay man, a straight man will hardly ever risk taking a chance that he is honing in on another man's territory, unless he is drunk or rude and if so, you don't want that man, anyway.

To put it bluntly, when you are out with any man, you significantly lower any chance that another man will approach you. Keep your time with your male friend (gay or straight) limited. Balance your time with him by going out alone, as this is when men feel most at ease and "safe" to approach you.

If you are best friends with a straight male, the relationship likely came together under unusual circumstances. Perhaps he dated a friend of yours, or you worked on a project together at the office or in a class. For whatever reason, the two of you never took steps to make it romantic, yet you're very compatible and truly are great friends.

On the old sitcom *Friends*, the characters Rachel and Joey exemplify the straight male-female friendship that became awkward when they started seeing each other romantically. The straight best friend is a problematic Consumer because there is a chance for something to shift and violá, you're suddenly Rachel and Joey without the comic relief. Not only might you lose this friendship, you also run the risk of losing your heart to a Consumer who is just passing time. If he didn't pursue you as more than a friend initially, he is a Consumer who will accept the sex, but have no thought of being more with you. Starting to have sex with him changes things for you, but changes absolutely nothing for him.

The Man as a Best Friend is not to be confused with a man who started out as a friend, but clearly and unequivocally showed you that he had interest in you for more than friendship *from the start*. If this is the case, and he has three or less on the List of Consumer Characteristics, then ask yourself if you can return the feelings. If you can, you may find yourself in the arms of a Buyer.

This most benign of the Toxic Consumers can fill your needs for companionship and friendship, while keeping you from meeting other men for potential romance and commitment. The degree to which this is possibly toxic is in direct proportion to the amount of time The Man as a Best Friend takes away from your dating and real possibilities for a Buyer to come into your life. For some women, The Man as a Best Friend takes years off their romantic life.

Be super honest with yourself if you are in a relationship with either one of these seemingly benign Consumers. Are you fulfilling your need for a male in your life with a gay or straight best friend to not deal with a man romantically and/or sexually? By giving you his male attention, conversation, interaction, and perhaps a little affection, is your gay or straight best friend becoming a substitute for a romantic relationship? If so, how can you step back? Take a closer look at both your own and your friend's motives. By changing the amount of time you are spending together, you'll favorably change the odds of finding a romantic partner.

2: The No-Try Guy

The No-Try Guy is a unique animal. No one can really figure him out. You might have become friends with him in college or on the job. Maybe he's a neighbor or the cousin of a friend. He is always polite and nice, if not perhaps just a bit of an enigma. He has never made a verbal or physical pass at you, talked about dates – male or female – and you've never seen him with anyone. Everything with Mr. No-Try is ambiguous.

There is a question as to whether or not this Consumer has feelings for you, but he's never indicated anything by word or action. Some friends question his sexuality because he has never put the moves on you. While he's similar to The Man as a Best Friend, you really don't feel close to or completely easy around Mr. No-Try. There is something about the relationship that feels false or phony if not a little forced. You may text and talk quite a bit and find yourself spending time with him only to feel empty afterwards, vowing not to see him as much.

At times, you wonder if there could be anything between you, but it is usually a thought you toss out quickly. It's as much of a puzzlement as to why you spend time with him as it is that he doesn't reveal much about himself or try to be physical with you. Whatever amount of time you are spending with this man, if you are without a significant other in your life, it's too much! This man is merely a Consumer minus the sex and/or the drive to try for more.

A former client of mine reported that her No-Try Guy would take her to every family gathering and out to nice dinners "every now and then." When she stated that he had been doing so for over a year, I was a bit taken aback. When I opened her eyes to the fact that he was a No-Try Consumer, she seemed a bit confused and dismayed.

I pointed out that this man was taking a great deal of her time and mental energy and asked why she would allow that to happen for so long. She admitted thinking that he might be interested "on some level," and that she didn't want to thwart "a chance" should that be the case. She stated that her Mr. No-Try was a "good guy with a good job," and that he "loved children." "Besides," she said, "I continue to date others occasionally so what's the harm?"

This client suffered from what I call the "good-on-paper syndrome." Her No-Try Guy seemed like a possibility in terms of his age, education, proximity, family, and desire to have children, but there was nothing more to this relationship than what looked good from the outside. Once I began pointing out all that could be going on with this Consumer – from being sexually dysfunctional, just not that into her, or being gay but not "out" with his family and friends – to having a girlfriend of whom his family wouldn't approve and for whom my client was an appropriate stand-in – my client began to see how she was wasting her precious time and attention on a man who had no intentions. Men who are interested make their intentions known! When they don't, don't waste your time!

3: The Friends With Benents

A relatively "new" Consumer on the scene of social acceptance in the last thirty years or so is The Friend with Benefits (FWB). Also known as The "Go-To" Guy, this man is always there for you when you need him, for sex that is. In all fairness, he can be there for a lot of other things, like fixing your garbage disposal as long as it doesn't take up too much of his time. The Friend with Benefits is generally a great guy who might have started as a friend and "yada, yada, yada," you're now having sex.

The FWB Consumer can also be a former boyfriend. You two had a great sex life, but your relationship was awful, so you decided it would be beneficial just to have what was good and "yada, yada, yada," you find yourself in this type of arrangement. While all seems harmless, someone is likely going to get hurt, and because of the male and female ways of attaching and loving, that someone is likely going to be you.

It may feel mature to make decisions about adult physical needs that avoid the emotional "stuff." The problem lies in the fact that the physical works perfectly for a man who doesn't connect sex and emotions or bond through time and sex, but is the worst thing for a woman who does both of these things naturally and biologically.

One recent study found the one thing that women wanted more than any other was to be desired. This explains the difficulties of purely sexual relationships. Women want to be desired for the whole of who they are, not just their physical being. When in a FWB relationship, a woman can become very confused. She knows she is liked (the man is her friend) and there are genuine feelings. The sex is pleasurable so she naturally bonds. This is confusing for her, but The FWB Consumer has the best of both worlds because for him there is sex with no bonding and no change in his feelings.

As a woman, you're the cute "puppy!" Don't let a FWB Consumer take you for a walk a few nights a week, then drop you off and leave you alone until he feels like coming back for another "once or twice" around the block. You're looking for a guy who is ready to "adopt," and once he finds you, he'll be anxious to take you home, give you all that you need, and have you with him every night. That's what should make you want to "wag your tail!"

Dating is not something that most people like very much. For most, it's a necessary evil toward finding love. Being open and available to meet and date takes a particular kind of energy and intention, which is partially driven by getting physical and emotional needs met. Men have this energy at the surface, and it's readily available to them all the time! For women, this energy can be easily defused by having the companionship and attention of men with whom they feel connected. For men who are looking, if they don't feel the right energy coming from you, they'll just pass you by. There is an old joke that goes something like:

"What does a man have to do to impress a woman on the first date?"

"Everything."

"And what does a woman have to do to impress a man on the first date?"

"Show up."

To this answer, in all seriousness, I would add, "and have the energy and essence of being free and available."

Being involved with a FWB Consumer, a No-Try Guy or The Man as a Best Friend can give a woman a feeling of being connected and even a false sense of being in a relationship. Your needs to connect to a man are temporarily filled which can feel better than having no connection at all. What ultimately feels best is being in a viable relationship. Don't short-change the process by short-changing yourself with a FWB Consumer and vice versa.

4: The Boy-Toy

Since the December-May romance between older women and younger men began to be statistically documented in the late 1980s (long after the movies *The Graduate* and *Harold and Maude,* in the late 1960s and early 1970s), this type of relationship has been, pardon the pun, on the rise. As with any other social phenomena that becomes commonplace, while seemingly a wonderful social leap, there are negatives for any woman who opts to be in the arms of a Boy-Toy Consumer.

While there is no real match for the high you'll be riding when pursued and wooed by a younger guy, ask yourself, at what expense? You may find that the boost to your confidence, libido, and joie-de-vivre isn't worth the trade-off for the time you're out of "the real" dating market because you're attached to someone who statistically will never commit.

It appears that slightly over 5% of wives are five years older than their husbands and only slightly over 1% are ten years older. This seems to correspond with the statistical fact that generally men aged forty and above marry women who are five to ten years younger. Translated, this means that younger men are not marrying older women in any significant numbers, and that the competition for age-appropriate men in the forty-plus age range for women is high. It's therefore wise for women over the age of forty who wish to have a committed partner in life not to waste their time with this particular Consumer.

No matter your age or his age, you, being female, bond through time and sex and he, being male, does not. This means that you have a much greater chance of losing your head in this relationship than he does. While knowing him in the biblical sense may be wondrous and wonderful, what is most important with this compelling and shiny "toy" is the ancient Greek adage, "Know thyself." If you are the rare woman who can overrule your heart with your head, then this Consumer may, in fact, be harmless and not as toxic as he could be to someone else who wouldn't be able to keep the statistical reality in her mind. Use your head for a moment, knowing that each moment that you are being consumed by a younger man, you are also keeping yourself from meeting and maybe matching with a potential age-appropriate Buyer. As we all know, there are exceptions to every rule, but as I remind my clients: You are an exceptional woman, but for the best chances of winning at love and romance, it's best not to think of yourself as the exception to the rule.

Jodi, a friend in her late forties, is one of the rare exceptions. She is divorced with teenaged children and says she has not wanted a relationship since the breakup of her marriage. Her divorce was quite contentious, and her husband was often controlling and belittling. Jodi has been in relationships with two younger men in the nine years following her divorce and each has made her quite happy. Both younger men were fun, kind, and loving. She stated that she liked not having to complicate her children's lives with another man besides their father and that she enjoyed keeping her romantic life private from all but her closest of female friends.

Jodi shared what allowed her to remain emotionally neutral. The young men with whom she became involved were more than ten years her junior. She stated that this allowed her head to "overrule" her heart with her head. One man was twelve years younger and the other was fourteen years younger. Jodi felt that had either of these very nice men been within a ten-year age difference, she would have likely been lulled into a "false sense" of real possibility with each. Instead, she said she was able to keep her head "on straight" and found that because she never wanted more than the men could offer, the relationships were both "satisfying, loving, and actually healing."

5: The Long-Distance Dude

The romance that swirls around The Long-Distance Dude during the initial stages when this man presents himself as a Buyer is blissful and yes, can be in*toxic*ating! Your meetings are filled with the best of what romance has to offer. You part without having to see or be around the unseemly or annoying habits of the other.

There are many reasons why this Consumer is high on the list of Toxic Consumers, as it is a universal truth that there is only one thing in the world that brings people together and more importantly, keeps them together: proximity. We can argue that with global transportation being as easy as it is, that we can change our definition of proximity. However, definitions, by definition, don't change!

As a dating and relationship coach, it is my belief that long-distance relationships don't work in the long run for one main reason, The Puppy Principle.

We've established that when a man meets a woman he wants to pursue, she will not know whether he is a potential Buyer or a Consumer. As a smart woman, she will play by The Rules for the best chance of having anything of substance materialize with a man – near or far. While The Rules will entice him, if a man doesn't get a consistent dose of "puppy love" from the "puppy" he loves because she is too far away, when another cute "puppy" crosses his path, he is inclined to follow her home for lots of petting and whatever other licks and tricks she'll give him.

If you happen to be with a Long-Distance Dude, take a long look at your situation from an objective distance. Did you establish a relationship when living near each other, and are you making plans to be together with a firm commitment in place? Or did you just happen to sit next to a man on a plane, spend two hours talking non-stop, and then "just happen" to have had an incredibly connected "lay-over?"

There are many possibilities and caveats that need to be accounted for with The Long-Distance Dude. If you met a on a tropical beach vacation and had a tantalizing tryst that you are now hoping will continue moving in the direction of a real relationship despite living a continent apart, be extra-strict with yourself and with him. Make him show himself to be a Buyer within the first few months of you both being home and back to your regular lives. If there are no tangible signs that the LDD wants to spend every other weekend together, accompanied by discussions of moving the two of you within close proximity in under a year's time, it might be best to keep your distance.

6: The Player

The Player is an Ultimate Consumer to which most all women have fallen prey at one time or another. He is second only to the Married Man and Damaged Consumer in terms of his toxicity; however, The Player may be equally as toxic as both, in that he has little to no understanding or compunction about what he does to women.

The Player takes the natural inclination of men to achieve a woman to a level akin to a sport. Never thinking about how his actions hurt women (or caring about it), The Player indulges his every whim, sparing no amount of time or money to get what he wants. The harder it is for The Player to "win," the more he wants to play until he does.

This Consumer will work until he completely wears down a woman's resolve. He will do all in his cunning power to make any woman he focuses on believe that he is enraptured by her in a way that he has "never" been with any other woman. Many Players believe this lie themselves, at least until they feel they've completed their quest to conquer.

The Player may be a serial Player and consume women one at a time, or juggle multiple women at once. Either way, he can never be without a woman, as a woman gives The Player a sense of self. The Player without female attention feels as though he is dying inside. The anxiety he experiences is unbearable, and he will pursue any woman who crosses his path, no matter her age or appropriateness. He knows little else besides the relief he feels from the high of pursuing women. Without a woman's attention, The Player loses all sense of identity. He is a man who has trouble being alone or without the company of a woman for even a short period of time.

Players are typically the easiest of all Consumers to identify. Many times, they have other addictions in addition to their addiction to women. They may be compulsive gamblers, sex/porn addicts, alcoholics, or drug-addicted. They may work out excessively or have a hobby that is flashy or showy to an extreme degree.

Players run the gamut of the amount of interest and investment in their careers and are rarely workaholic, instead preferring the high they get from their activities or addictions such as gambling or substances. Workaholism is typically more of an escape mechanism than an actual addiction, and therefore it doesn't fulfill the need for thrills and distraction that The Player requires.

Most women who have ever fallen prey to The Player, even if they found themselves heartbroken, are able to get over this Consumer rather quickly. This is due to the fact that in hindsight, most women can recognize that the man is a Player and simply thank the heavens that they escaped. Since a relationship with The Player is typically quite shallow as well as short-lived, this also makes it easier for a woman to move on and not look back.

If you find yourself falling victim to Players more than once or twice, this is something you'll want to explore. You may be thrill-seeking or afraid of a committed relationship yourself, and The Player can be the easiest and most available man for a rollercoaster ride. With its short highs and lows with little in between, the ride with The Player is certainly a thrill for a while, but it always stops short and when you step off, it usually leaves you feeling dizzy and just a little bit queasy.

7: The Married Man

The Married Man is a particularly egregious type of Toxic Consumer, as he is a man who has proven that he is capable of commitment, albeit to someone else. This ability, coupled with the intensity with which a married man will exhibit his true feelings of longing for a woman who makes him feel desire and desirable, can be difficult to forego. But forego you must. Remember that the capability of this Married Man to commit only goes so far or else he would not be contemplating or cultivating encounters with another woman.

As many smart and savvy women will tell you, as a general rule, the old adage about dating the spouse of another is true: "Men don't leave their wives." You'll find out why this is in Chapter 8. For now, if you haven't, be sure not to fall prey to The Married Man's consumeristic tales of longing, woe, and being "misunderstood." You are an exceptional woman. Regarding The Married Man, statistics show that you have little chance of being "the exception to the rule," however. With few exceptions, you'll have nothing beyond empty promises and holidays alone for as long as you are with The Married Man.

8: The Damaged Consumer

The Damaged Consumer comes in all shapes, sizes, and ages, as well as in all educational, vocational, and socioeconomic statuses. This tumult of toxicity runs the gamut from being a relatively stable guy who has been unable to handle being hurt by the females of his past to being a truly dysfunctional or perhaps even mentally disordered man.

One reason The Damaged Consumer is the worst of Consumers, surpassing even The Married Man, is that he is single and therefore, by default, available. Unlike The Player, Mr. Damaged actually derives something from being in a relationship with one woman and, in many cases, is not willing to let go or allow the woman to move on even if he no longer wants her.

This Consumer can be downright obsessive and controlling. He can be unwittingly manipulative and completely lacking in insight – or worse, he just doesn't care about knowingly using a woman for his own pleasure and satisfaction. While The Player finds satisfaction in conquering and then quickly moving on, The Damaged Consumer can derive pleasure in staying and even greater satisfaction in keeping a woman connected and hooked.

Dianne's Damaged Consumer

Dianne came to me in great distress over a man with whom she had fallen in love. Her friend, Carmen, who I had helped to get back with a boyfriend who had left her without warning, referred Dianne. Using the approaches and strategies that can turn a Mr. Mixed Messages or a Prospective Buyer into a Bona Fide Buyer, Carmen was able to get her ex back, and in three months' time, she was enjoying a greatly improved relationship. Most importantly, Carmen was feeling valued and honored in a way she had "never experienced." Dianne wanted to see if, by working with me, it would be possible for her to have a similar outcome as Carmen and an improved relationship with her boyfriend, Baran.

In our correspondence to schedule our first call, Dianne stated that she was finally ready to "do something" and would gladly "try anything" I suggested. I sent Dianne my questionnaire as well as the Consumer vs. Buyer Relationship Test to get a deeper understanding of her relationship, and we scheduled an appointment for the following week.

The history that I reviewed prior to speaking to Dianne indicated that she had been with her boyfriend Baran for over 4 years. The Consumer vs. Buyer Relationship Test revealed Baran as a mid-range Ultimate Consumer. The two had met at a charity event where Baran had donated one of his paintings. Dianne had written that Baran had swept her off her feet in the first few months they were together and how she had never before experienced such sexual passion. "I thought I was pretty experienced," she wrote. "I never imagined there was so much to sex and a physical relationship – it was like the most powerful drug ever!"

It was clear from the details of Dianne's history with Baran that she had given a great deal of herself to a man who, with the exception of the first few months, gave little in return. Dianne confessed that she felt foolish having let the relationship "deteriorate into what it's become," but she told herself that Baran must have "strong feelings" for her, or he "would have broken it off."

Dianne felt that she and Baran were compatible in very important areas of life, as well as sharing an intense physical chemistry. They both had not been married and neither had children. Both were extremely independent and enjoyed the same taste in art and love of cultural events. Each year, they took short vacations to Europe to explore various cities and visit art museums. They shared a love of animals, and in one of Baran's more generous moods, he agreed to share the care of a cat that the two adopted from a friend of Dianne's.

During our first call, I was struck by how strongly and confidently Dianne presented herself. Dianne's written history with Baran indicated a woman more likely to be somewhat mild and soft-spoken. I asked Dianne to tell me more about her life with Baran over the last four years, and as she spoke, her strong voice became weaker as her emotions rose to the surface.

"I just love him," she stated. "I just want to make him happy, and it seems nothing I do is ever right or good enough." Dianne told me how Baran's moods would swing from completely sullen to elated and that, on occasion, he "actually seemed to care" and would be sensitive to her emotions. Dianne reported on Baran's need to smoke marijuana daily and while she was not clear on any of the details, she said that Baran had done a great deal of harder drugs in his youth. Whenever she had tried to ask about his past, Baran would curtly cut her off, saying "I tell you what it is I feel you should know."

With each passing encounter, from meeting his artist friends to spending time at his studio watching Baran create his enormous paintings, Dianne fell more and more in love. She described it as a wild ride that she couldn't just step off, but she also admitted that after four years, she was depleted and exhausted from not getting any "real love" from this intense and "emotionally closed-off" man.

Dianne, who was forty-three, told me that Baran, now in his mid-fifties, had spent much of his young adulthood "finding himself as an artist." He lived a bohemian lifestyle throughout his twenties and at the age of thirty-two, inherited a great deal of money from his grandfather. It was then that he came to the United States and after a gallery took him on, he began working with designers, creating paintings that were acquisitioned for lobbies and meeting rooms of large corporate clients.

Dianne stated that Baran, while hedonistically passionate, had never been consistently loving or affectionate. After the first few months, he stopped showing interest in Dianne and only begrudgingly agreed to join her at her family and social functions when he was "up to it." When the two talked about anything of relevance, Baran tended to be condescending. Dianne said that most of the time, he was simply avoidant. Dianne stated that during their years together, she took Baran on as a kind of "mission," because she saw his innate beauty and sensitivity and believed that her unconditional love could help him to blossom into the incredible man he was destined to be.

By the time she came to me, Dianne was depleted. She had tried everything and admitted being "emotionally exhausted" from giving her all and getting nothing in return. She was distraught at having "wasted so many good years" of her life, thinking she could fix things with Baran, because there was such chemistry and connection between them. While she felt "ashamed" that she was still with this man, she also stated that she simply couldn't tear herself away.

Dianne's family and friends were frustrated and confounded that such a lovely, smart woman would allow herself to be marginalized and treated so poorly. Dianne said she managed her own turmoil and confusion by attributing Baran's behavior to his "different culture and artistic soul." She also admitted staying because she felt that she was not going to find anyone else at this stage in her life who was as charismatic, interesting, and as physically appealing to her as Baran.

Dianne was caught in the trap of loving a Damaged Consumer. Upon our working together, and Dianne coming to terms with Baran's Consumer vs. Buyer Test Score, she began to accept that this man's dismissive behavior and occasional verbal abuse had nothing to do with any cultural differences or the fact that he was an artist. She started facing the fact that she may never know what is at the root or main cause of Baran's mood swings and emotional distancing.

Women are natural nurturers. Dianne was no exception. She was in love and felt that if she attended to Baran's wounds, she could help him, and he would love her for that. Whenever Baran would go missing for weeks at a time, Dianne would accept him back readily and easily, feeling that she was caretaking to his emotional turmoil. Worst of all, she would break up with him in fits of tears and frustration only to go running back to him when she could no longer handle his silence. None of Dianne's attempts at meaningful discussion of their relationship were tolerated by Baran. Instead, he addressed Dianne's emotions by "making love" to her.

When they were "coasting along," as Dianne put it, she tried to please Baran by making herself completely available and not doing anything to upset him. Despite intellectually understanding the dysfunction of continuing to stay, Dianne's relationship with Baran was a familiar, natural emotional place for her to be. She had never received any real attention or overt affection from her father and Baran felt "known" and comfortable.

Because of her constant pleasing behavior, Baran never had to wonder about or long for Dianne. I believe this lack of longing caused Baran to never fall in love with Dianne. Giving a man what he wants when he wants it and how it wants it doesn't work well under the best of circumstances. When dealing with a Damaged Consumer, it is particularly toxic.

Giving up needing to know what was happening with Baran was the first thing Dianne had to tackle for herself. Needing to know if Baran had an underlying mental health issue, had a traumatic childhood, or was seriously affected by the hard drug use in his past was not going to be useful to Dianne. Once she accepted what Baran was *showing* her, telling her, and (not) giving her, rather than what her excuses for his behavior gave her permission to do, she began to accept the reality of this man and their relationship.

I knew by Baran's score and Dianne's reports, that Baran was not merely an Ultimate Consumer, but a Damaged Consumer. I also knew Dianne would need to make every attempt possible to see if Baran could have a change of heart for her to heal. This prompted Dianne to come to me, and I honored her desire and decision. Dianne was aware of the facts, but felt she needed to make every possible effort to make it work by utilizing the approaches and strategies that work time after time for other women, as was the case with her friend Carmen. While continually cautioning Dianne that her attempts would likely make little difference, I supported and guided her in strategies so that in the end, she would be able to comfort herself with knowing that she had tried everything possible for the best chance of success.

It was a difficult road, with one step forward and two steps back, but with support, Dianne started to apply the approaches and strategies that have shifted Prospective Buyers, Bona Fide Buyers, and even Mixed-Messages Consumers to committing. Most importantly, in the process, Dianne felt empowered and began to get back to the strongest version of herself. She was able to admit that she had allowed Baran to "belittle and breakdown" her sense of self-worth and self-esteem. In just three months, Dianne was able to completely end the negative cycle of consumerism to which she had fallen victim.

Baran rarely stepped out of his behavioral pattern during those three months. As an Ultimate and Damaged Consumer, this was not at all surprising. When Dianne stopped making the overtures and efforts, Baran simply didn't respond in all but two instances. When he did reach out to her on those rare occasions, Dianne was able to see the completely self-serving, sexual nature of the attempts. Her renewed sense of self-worth allowed Dianne to forego her natural inclination and temptation to cater to Baran's needs and to focus more on her own. While it took time and work to accept the loss of the "what if" with Baran, Dianne felt empowered to have taken the steps to work with a coach and put an end to the damaging and unfulfilling relationship.

As a postscript, through our continued work, Dianne slowly started to date again. She rejoined the online dating site where she had met Baran nearly five years earlier, and she joined new sites. We tweaked her profile, and I coached Dianne on the ways to deal with men and present herself so as not to play into the consumerism that is rampant online. With the effective approaches and strategies around texting, taking calls, and answering online inquiries, Dianne began to date a man who is showing desire for who she is and not just for her body. She is making this new man wonder and working The Rules to keep herself from giving in to his needs in the knee-jerk fashion that was her pattern. She recently stated that she finds being thought of and treated well refreshing and that she "could really get used to it!"

The Rules Effect

Every day in my practice, I see The Rules at work. The list of books, by Ellen Fein and Sherrie Schneider are referenced at the end of this book. I recommend that every woman read *Not Your Mother's Rules* to start. There is no better tool for a woman to feel empowered and knowledgeable in her dating life than The Rules.

Dianne began reading *The Rules* and found me via The Rules website. Once she had extricated herself from the hold that Baran had on her and began on-line dating, her practice of The Rules helped to keep her on a clear path and value herself, once again. It helped Dianne to read the list of Rules as a type of mantra. As we worked together, we focused most specifically on my Receive-Retreat-Respond method, and she felt supported to maintain her resolve.

I find that there is an added benefit to The Rules for women to consider, that men ultimately gain a great deal from women practicing The Rules. The Rules make men crave women who practice them because The Rules provide men the opportunity to feel love that some say they've "never felt."

In speaking to men, I hear how much they long to find a woman who inspires them like no other, a woman who makes them work to achieve her time, attention, and affection. Following The Rules puts women in the driver's seat of their relationships. Once a man shows himself to be fully committed and in love (a Bona Fide Buyer), a woman is then free to make her decision about that man, according to her feelings of love for him.

Chapter Seven

The Buyers – The Good, the Better, and the Best

J ust by virtue of being a woman, you've likely had your share of heartache from Consumers. From the charismatic and sexy Player who hooked you just to have his fun and flee in a month, to the wonderful Mixed-Messages Consumer to whom you gave more than a few years of your life – loving him and trying to make him see the light – and all variations thereof. Yes, there are three things on which all women can count on in life: Death, taxes and Consumers!

But along with the Consumers, you've likely also had several Buyers cross your path and, for one reason or another, something happened to cause you or the Buyer to stumble and not complete the journey to a lifetime of love and commitment.

You've previously reviewed the List of Consumer Characteristics that outline a man's state when not ready, willing, or able to commit. Now, we'll look at the Buyers and discuss what it takes for a man to go the distance and bond to a woman he loves.

A Man Is in the State of Being a Buyer When He:

- Has achieved his educational, career or avocational goals or believes he will be able to achieve them while in a relationship.

- Has fulfilled the single-life experiences he wants to have had before settling down with one woman.

- Feels confident he can be faithful.

- Is financially successful or stable enough to meet his responsibilities with little fear of failure.

- Is in love.

The Prospective Buyer (60 – 90 Score)

The Prospective Buyer is a man who doesn't give you any mixed messages. While he's not 100% sure of his readiness or willingness to make a long-term commitment, he is consistent in his love for you and shows himself to be able to be a committed partner. Most importantly, he is interested in you for more than just what you give to him in the moment.

The Prospective Buyer is either a Consumer who is good at hiding his mixed emotions, or he currently has too many reservations about your relationship, his freedom needs, or his achievement level to have scored higher. A Prospective Buyer may be wrestling with concerns that he is likely not disclosing to you, but there is definitely something that is not quite lined up for him to be in the next category, The Bona Fide Buyer. Don't make the mistake of believing that your Prospective Buyer "just hasn't had enough time to decide." Remember:

Time is Not a Factor in Determining a Man's Readiness, Willingness, or Ability to Commit.

If you've made up your mind that you wish to have this prospect as your life partner, you might find yourself fluctuating between being complacent and feeling like your relationship is in the bag or running high with anxiety, trying to prove your worth and value to him, in order to transform him into a Bona Fide Buyer.

Balance, calm, and supreme confidence are required to see this man move up the scale. Once scored in this range, it's best to make it a short-time period of instituting simple, effective strategies that will ignite a Prospective Buyer's desire to lockdown a committed relationship with you. Without the effective and meaningful ways of being and relating to a Prospective Buyer, time will pass, and his interest may simply smolder or, worse, cool off for good.

How Time Factors In (Not!)

Time has meaning, value, and significance to women in terms of relationships. Women become nostalgic about months or years with their significant others and mark time in their relationships:

"This is our *second* Valentine's Day."

"This is the *fourth* dinner we've had with his parents."

"We make breakfast together *every Sunday* morning."

"We've been going there together *for years.*"

Until they've made a formal commitment, men don't think about their relationships in terms of time. This is because until men make a formal commitment, they are not bonded to a woman. Only when a man makes a formal commitment that bonds him to a woman will he begin to think about his relationship as part of his life's achievements.

Why is this relevant in speaking about The Prospective Buyer? Because the amount of time spent with a Prospective Buyer or any man, without getting to a formal commitment, is directly counter to getting a commitment for the long run. In other words, the longer you continue in a relationship without it being formalized through a man deciding to commit, the less likely a man is to do so.

**Women Bond Through Time and Sex.
Men Bond by Living Up to Their Decisions,
Commitments, and Responsibilities.**
#5 of Coach Paula's List of Gender Gaps

Ever wonder why it's so commonplace for a man to be in a relationship or live with a woman for years or even decades only to leave her and marry someone else? Have you also wondered why it is that the old adage "men don't leave their wives" is also (statistically) true? The way men bond in relationships explains this quite easily.

Cracking the Bonding Code

I pay great thanks to licensed professional counselor and mature, married (and thus, bonded) man Bob Grant, LPC. Mr. Grant theorizes that men bond to women in only one way, by making a commitment. I wholeheartedly agree. I further believe that to truly bond, a man needs to *decide* to make a *formal* commitment, whereby he announces to the world and to himself that he is making the decision to take on the responsibility he believes commitment to be. Living together, as it is done in most cases, where there is no formal or legal announcement, contract or ceremony, does not provide what a man needs to be formally committed and thus, truly bonded.

Not a Ball and Chain, Just a Leash

Remember when you were taking care of Scout for me? You were enjoying your time with him, and you loved him. You weren't willing to take him as your own and commit to him because you were not ready and willing to take on the responsibility of him or of any puppy. You didn't feel able to take Scout as your own because of your finances and the changes you saw ahead of you, like moving, switching jobs, and traveling. But let's say for the sake of argument that when I asked you to take Scout, you decided to accept the responsibility.

You said yes, and I dropped Scout off with his bed, food, sweaters, toys, leashes, collars, and anything else I thought you might need to take care of him. I gave you his latest shot reports and the number of the veterinarian he's seen in the past. We sealed the deal and I cried as I kissed him goodbye. He went over to his favorite spot on your floor, lied down, and made himself at home. He looked up at you, lovingly panting away. Scout is now yours.

You would likely go about your day and nothing will have felt all that different. For a while, the transition wouldn't seem that noticeable because your commitment to Scout made no logistical change in your hour-to-hour activities or routine.

Logistically, things would be much the same as when you took care of Scout for me on the weekends. But despite the similarity to all that you've previously experienced with Scout, something now feels a little special.

During walks, you find yourself telling the neighbors and store owners that you adopted Scout (committed to him). You stop at the pet shop and buy a special collar that is more to your taste, and you enjoy putting it around his neck, marking the commitment in an "official" way. On Monday, you call the veterinarian and explain that Scout is now yours. You make sure the vet has all your information and ask about getting a microchip ID for him because you like to let him run off-leash when you go to the beach and on hikes. You also get Scout's exact birth date, so you can celebrate it.

Each action subsequent to your decision reinforces your commitment and creates a bond to Scout that was previously missing. While you don't love him any more than you did when you took care of him for me, you now love him a little differently. You are now bonding with Scout because of the decision you made. Even though you were reluctant to take him, once you made the decision to make him your responsibility, you followed through on the commitment and now you are bonding to him.

While walking Scout through the park, you picture what the future will be like for you with him as he ages. You think about what will happen if he ever gets sick and who you'll ask to take care of him when you travel. You think of the date you accepted my proposal and mark that as your "anniversary." Scout is now totally *your* love and *your* responsibility!

Your friends and family are so happy that you have a companion. They were worried you wouldn't ever adopt a furry friend that you love and are thrilled you committed to doing so! What happens when Scout misbehaves, annoys you, or poops on the carpet? Do you toss him out or want to return him? Do you think about taking him to a shelter and leaving him there? Of course not.

While you might get angry if Scout chews an expensive pair of shoes, you don't simply shirk your responsibility. Because he is now yours and yours alone, you start to bond with Scout, and it will take more than feelings of anger or disappointment for you to do anything as big as reneging on the commitment you made. For all but the most egregious of reasons, you commit to Scout for a lifetime and don't ever consider giving him away just because there are times when you don't like him very much, he acts up, or costs you a fortune. You took on a responsibility and you're going to live up to it, even when you don't much feel like it!

This is what a man does when he makes a romantic commitment. While you bond because of your feelings, a man bonds through his decision-making related to what he sees as a responsibility. Just as you could love any puppy and mind it for a friend for as long as the friend will let you, you only bond to the pet to whom you commit. Most importantly, you committed via a decision, and once made, you do all in your power to live up to that decision no matter your negative feelings from time to time.

No matter his feelings, a man will live
by his decisions in order to show the world
that he doesn't make bad decisions and
that he is not a failure.

Failure is Not an Option

A man fills his identity needs from "sucking it up" in a bad situation once he has formally committed. Once a man makes a formal decision of which the world, loved ones, and friends are made aware, failure is no longer an option he will consider. To a man, failure means he is not competent to make good decisions – or worse, that he acts "like a girl" and reneges on decisions because of his feelings. To a man, failure means that he can't control his life and his environment. Failure means he does not have the mental strength to handle difficulty. Failure means he is weak in his resolve to "stick things out" when the going gets tough. Failure means he is not much of a man. This resistance to what men perceive as failure is why 80% of divorces are initiated and brought to the courts by women. Men don't want to fail or look like wimps who abandon their commitments, and if a man fails, he certainly doesn't want that failure to be public.

In the next chapter, you'll find out why it is that statistically a man will cheat on his wife and not leave her, even if he loves the woman with whom he is cheating more than he loves his wife. For now, let's celebrate the resolve of men and give credit where credit is due. Let's be thankful that men live by, and want to live up to, their decisions! It's why we want so much for the man we love to make a decision to commit! It's why we want a man to be a Bona Fide Buyer.

The Bona Fide Buyer (91 – 106 Score)

If your man has scored in this category, there are few if any questions about his feelings for you and desire to be with you. What you won't know with absolute certainty is where your guy is with the other four items on the List of Buyer Characteristics. It's likely, however, that a man who scores as a Bona Fide Buyer is in a pretty good place with all items on the list. Regardless, if he hasn't locked this relationship down, there is something he is struggling with, either in himself, about the relationship, or about you.

When a man decides, there is usually little to no wavering. Once the decision is made, a man lets it be known to all in his orbit. Therefore, no matter how connected and loving the relationship feels to you, until you have a *formal* commitment, your Bona Fide Buyer has some reservation. His hesitation could be any number of things that have nothing to do with you, or something about you, despite loving you, that he feels unable to voice. Many men who find themselves in this situation run or even hide, rather than face a woman directly.

Working on the approaches and strategies that allow your Bona Fide Buyer to disclose to you what his hesitation may be, without you overtly asking, is very useful. The subtle strategies tailored specifically to the details of your relationship are what will help an otherwise languishing-in-limbo live-in situation, to move up to a joyful joint lifetime venture! If you're with a Bona Fide Buyer who hasn't taken things to the next level, reading *The Rules for Marriage* is a great place to start. More support may be needed, but utilizing The Rules for those in fully committed relationships can be very helpful to kick things off – possibly for next wedding season!

Chapter Eight
The Play Book – Putting It All Together on the Field

There is great news for women considering marriage! Statistically, men don't leave. While the reports from divorcestatistics.org list 41% of first marriages ending in divorce, 60% of second marriages ending in divorce, and 73% of third marriages ending in divorce, 80% of the time it was the woman who filed for the divorce.

The fact that 80% of divorces are filed by women reveals to some degree that if a woman wants to stay and work on a marriage in some fashion, the man will likely or at least try to do so. While certainly the reasons are multifactorial, my Sports Supposition explains why only 20% of the time it's the man who seeks a divorce. If even only somewhat statistically valid, it means that getting to an "I do" may not be a bad idea for a woman who wants to have a man who is committed to her, until such time/if ever, she decides that she no longer wants the partnership.

The Sports Supposition

Most women live by the conventional wisdom of not getting involved with a married man. This is not only due to the moral, ethical and religious or social reasons, but also because it is well known that married men don't leave their wives. As a dating and relationship coach, many women come to me and ask why, in this day and age when divorce is so prevalent, it still seems to be (and statistically is) the case. I generally sum it up in five words:

Men Don't Leave Their Team.

Think of any adult male you know, married or otherwise. He likely has a team that he follows for various sports. No matter how badly his team performs and how much the man pays lip service to hating "those losers," "those bums," or whatever choice words he may have for them when they fumble, miss a shot or lose, he never stops rooting for them. He doesn't suddenly say, "You know, the Knicks haven't won an NBA Championship in forty years, so I guess I'll find another team." Not only will a man not leave the team he supports, he will not leave his own team. Think about an adult male you know who plays on an amateur team – or better yet, give a man the hypothetical below and see how he answers you. Let's give the man in our hypothetical the name Tom.

At the "Root" of the Home Team

Tom, aged forty-five, plays on an adult baseball team. He's been on the team for nearly twenty years, but he is tired of leaving work early to make it to practice on time or getting up for games on Saturday morning. He started to become disenchanted with the coach somewhere around the third year of being on the team. For Tom, it was then that being committed to the practice and game schedule and following the coach's rules, began to get old and became more of a chore than a joy. At the end of the second season, Tom told his friend, "I guess the honeymoon is over!" While initially he thought the coach was cool, in reality, dealing with him over the years completely turned Tom off. Tom complains that the coach no longer allows him to play third base as much, and he doesn't put him up at bat very often, either. Tom is bored and frustrated.

Despite being unhappy, playing on this team and becoming disenchanted with his coach, Tom still loves the game. It's just not as much fun for him to play on this old team. He complains to his friends and the guys at work about the practice times, the controlling coach, Saturday games, and his minor aches after practice. Throughout the years, Tom's friend has suggested he speak with the coach or just turn in his glove and retire his number. Does Tom quit?

You may be thinking, of course, why would Tom stay with something that clearly frustrates and bores him, takes his time and energy, and that he no longer enjoys?

Men Stick It Out

Tom stays because he is a man. If he were to simply quit, to his buddies, his teammates, and most importantly, to himself, he would be labeled or would label himself as a quitter. The unspoken man-code states that a man doesn't shirk his responsibilities just because he no longer "feels like" living up to his commitments. A real man "sucks it up" and "sticks it out" until the bitter end.

Tom's coach is sick of trying to make it work. When in one of his better moods, he allowed Tom to play third base, gave him more time off than his teammates, and tried talking to him about his attitude. Tom will continue to make it miserable for everyone including himself, but he won't leave. Instead, he argues with the coach until the coach gets so fed up that he kicks Tom off the team for his bad attitude and lack of interest in playing to make the team a winner.

Take the challenge and give three adult men this hypothetical about Tom. If your experience is like mine, at a minimum, two out of the three men will tell you that Tom doesn't quit. I usually receive an immediate and unequivocal "no way" from every man I ask the question "Does Tom quit?"

It's simply not part of male human nature to make a commitment and then renege on it simply because it's no longer satisfying, fun or feels good. Once committed to something where a man has made a decision and given his word, he doesn't just quit, leave or (statistically) initiate divorce. Men don't leave their team, and as a man's wife, you are his team.

My Sports Supposition explains why, at least from a biological and anthropological vantage point, men stay with their wives despite being unhappy and dissatisfied. Of course, there are all manner of financial, logistical, and other factors that come into play, but the fact that 80% of divorces are filed by women is rooted in something deep within males to "stick it out."

Strike 3? Not Me!

Women want more out of life than a man who stays married merely out of obligation and commitment, but refuses to work on the emotional or sexual part of a relationship. Women live by their feelings, can accept they made a mistake, and want themselves and the people they love to be the happiest, connected, and most emotionally fulfilled they can be. Men stay to prove their decisions were right, and that they don't renege on their commitments or responsibilities. It's typically not until the bitter end – and usually an ultimatum – that a man will agree to go to couples counseling to better a relationship. Most of the time, for women, it's too little, too late.

In our hypothetical, if Tom just quits his team, to his buddies and teammates and to himself, he would be weak and a real "girl" for getting upset at not being given the positions he wants or not getting up to bat as often as he'd like. He'd also be letting down the guys who are expecting him to be there to support them. "Good men" don't do that to their teammates, buddies, family, wives, or children. Tom made a decision twenty years ago, and he is going to remain responsible to that decision no matter how miserable he is or how miserable he makes the team. Tom keeps going to bat until the bitter end, and he will do anything not to strike out!

You may be thinking, ok, while a man won't leave a team or a relationship, it's often the case that he will cheat on his wife. What about that? To that I say yes, you are absolutely right!

Stealing Bases

So why would a man be okay with cheating after he is bonded through marriage? We understand that Tom doesn't quit his team because he lives by his decisions, commitments and responsibilities. This doesn't mean, however, that Tom doesn't *feel* unhappy!

Tom is completely unhappy. While Tom dislikes the coach, the control of the practice times, the game schedule, and the one position he is forced to play, Tom still loves the game of baseball! Tom's love of the game may cause him to find another team that he likes better! He finds a team a few towns over that entices him with fun and being up at bat a lot more times in a few months than the coach has let him in years!

Tom is very excited by this new team, as it feels relaxing to be away from the pressures and boredom of the home team. The coach on the new team entices Tom to come and play "whenever he wants" and makes little to no demands on him – at first. Tom gets to play positions he hasn't played in years and feels like a twenty-year old again!

The new team has gone so far as to promise they won't tell anyone that Tom is playing with them. Tom is elated. No one on the home team will know he is cheating with another team! He stays with his old team, shows himself to be a responsible player, and is on his best behavior with the home coach.

Tom feels that by getting his needs met elsewhere, he can even be nicer to the home coach! By playing on the team a few towns over, Tom feels everyone on the home team is happier. While he may feel a bit guilty, guilt is preferable to being seen as a quitter. By playing on the new team, Tom gets to play the game as he wants to play it, and he doesn't have to feel like a failure for not living up to his responsibility and commitment he made to the home team.

Tom manages his intermittent pangs of guilt by telling himself that he is doing the right thing by remaining "loyal" to the home team. He also justifies his actions by telling himself that he deserves to play on the new team because he has been unhappy with the home team for many years, though never discussed his unhappiness with the coach.

Because men view women, love, and commitment so very differently, they can believe that cheating is somewhat harmless and much preferable to reneging on their commitments. As men bond only by making a commitment, a cheating husband does not feel that being with another woman breaks the bond to his wife. Because he isn't reneging on the commitment, he doesn't feel he is breaking the bond! To a wife, who bonds through time and sex, a cheating husband is typically the ultimate betrayal. As a woman views commitment through a lens of love and feelings, to her, a man breaks a bond merely by *feeling* that he wants to be with another woman!

When the Coach Steps Off the Field

You might be thinking, what happens if the wife is the one that cheats? A man certainly feels like the bond is broken then, correct? Again, you are absolutely right!

While a man feels betrayed when a wife cheats, it's not quite the same feeling that a woman feels when she has been the victim of cheating. While equally horrible, each gender experiences a different type of pain when betrayed in a love relationship. Complex and contextual, men have a hard time explaining why a woman cheating on them is "the worst thing" a man can experience. Much the same as how a woman cannot convey to a man that sex is not merely a physical act and that for women, there is almost always residual feelings related to having sex, men feel that women can't quite understand the experience of their wife or serious love interest cheating on them.

To understand the differences in how men and women experience infidelity, it's important to go back to the basics of men and women. To make it easy for my clients to remember, I tell them to "think three." Three C's, that is.

The Three Cs for Women:
Women are Intrinsically about Cooperating, Connecting, and Caretaking.

The Three Cs for Men:
Men are Intrinsically about Challenge, Competition, and Conquering.

If her man is unfaithful, a woman will tend to feel that the special love and *connection* the couple shared was betrayed. When a woman is unfaithful, a man will tend to feel that his woman betrayed him by allowing a *challenger* or *competitor* into a space that he claimed and *conquered*.

While a man's infidelity causes a woman to feel complex emotions related to herself and her *relationship*, infidelity generally causes a man to feel that he might not measure up or be good enough in some tangible way. He will likely believe he is not pleasing his woman sexually or being a good enough provider. A man does not usually relate infidelity to the dynamics of the relationship. He does not usually consider that his partner may not be fulfilled emotionally and longs for connection, but rather he sees cheating as the ultimate challenge to an achievement he feels he conquered and would never be confronted on or forced to defend again.

Winning the Game

In no way am I condoning, justifying or pardoning men (or women) who cheat. I'm merely outlining the way in which many men frame their cheating as actually living up to the commitments they've made, borne from their decisions. While women feel heartbroken, disappointed, and in every way violated by a husband who cheats, the husbands who do, often believe the worst thing they could do is to renege on their decision to be responsible to the women to whom they committed.

Women who have been cheated on by their husbands would much prefer the men shirk their responsibility in favor of emotional and sexual truth and honesty. Many times, cheating men don't understand the outrage that their wives feel and in many cases, try to lessen incidents of infidelity as "not meaning anything" or saying, "it was just sex." Due to The Puppy Principle, in a great deal of one-time infidelities, this is actually the case for men. Sex for men can carry no meaning or feelings at all beyond the physical pleasure. This fact can be extremely disconcerting and disheartening to many women who cannot imagine a disconnect between love and sex. In relation to a long-term marriage, if a one-time infidelity can be seen by a wife in this light, many relationships cannot only be saved, but improved greatly through the emotional honesty that can arise in the man because of it.

80/20 Rules!

If you're thinking about our hypothetical and the chance of our teammate Tom leaving his wife to be with the other woman, statistically, that won't be happening. While Tom's wife will likely be one of the 80% filing for divorce, Tom has almost no statistical chance of marrying his mistress. According to Dr. Jan Halper's study of over 4,100 cheating men, only 3% of them divorced their wives and married their lovers.

Tom is much more likely to do all he can to make it up to his wife and to prove himself to be a better man and capable of living up to his decision and commitments in a way that will please her. Most typically, he will strive to prove his decision to marry his wife was right, that he is not a failure, and that he can go the distance on his commitment to her, no matter how hard it is or what he feels. While occasionally a cheating husband will leave his wife, 80% of the time, the wife will be the one making the decision about the direction of the marriage and deciding if she wants to attempt to work on the marital issues and stay.

Once a wife decides she wants a divorce, in most cases, the cheating man is typically no longer interested in the other woman for more than assuaging his feelings of hurt and failure. His main focus is, once again, achieving that which he valued enough to commit to in the first place. When a man strikes out with all the bases loaded, he will then step up to the plate and agree to work on the emotional/physical aspects of his marriage, should his coach be willing to give him another chance at bat.

A Case for Marriage

As you now know, women bond through time and sex. If a woman likes a man enough to spend some time and has satisfying sex with him, she will bond. She doesn't need a formal commitment or contract to be forever faithful in mind, body, and soul. She will give of herself and be responsible to her man in all ways without any formal occasion, contract, or ceremony. While the day in a white dress is wonderful, memorable, and meaningful, it's not at all necessary for a woman to be fully committed and bonded to a man she loves.

As men only bond only through making a formal commitment, as in marriage or some other formalized ceremony or celebration signifying a man taking responsibility in somewhat of a public manner, a commitment event is very important. This public ceremonious activity, no matter how small or informal, is the equivalent of a man getting his uniform and becoming part of a team. Once he is "suited up" with his number and it's official, statistically it is very unlikely that he will just walk off or quit.

If a woman commits to doing The Rules in dating and marries a man who ultimately cherishes and values her, if she continues with The Rules for marriage, she is less likely to have to face the possibility of infidelity. Because doing The Rules is such a rigorous vetting process for a man to be part of "the team" he is vying to be on, he values his spot on the team more so than he would if he were just allowed to walk on the field and play however he chooses. If the latter is the case, it's usually that he doesn't much care to secure a spot, as he doesn't value the team as a winner in the league, and worthy of his hard-won commitment. Additionally, and most importantly, The Rules make a man cherish and value "the coach." Once he is accepted as part of a team that plays by the rules, and the man knows that the coach doesn't accept anything less than good behavior and full-commitment to the game, he is much more apt to go the distance, and continue to keep proving himself to be first string in the coach's eyes and heart.

Adam Up at Bat

My client, Andie, is a single mom in her early forties. She divorced her first husband nearly fifteen years ago and has one daughter who is soon to be a teenager. Although quite religious, Andie told me that she never considered marrying again, as she felt there was "no need," as long as she could be in a "committed long-term partnership."

Andie contacted me in February of 2016 after dating a man she had met online and known for about four months. She was starting to fall for this man and wanted to ensure the best possibility of a long-term relationship. Utilizing a combination of The Rules and my advance/retreat strategies to incite wonder and longing in a man, Andie found herself enjoying a great relationship in which she was cherished, respected, and loved.

Andie took the Consumer vs. Buyer Relationship Test. Adam scored as a Bona Fide Buyer. I recall the session when I asked Andie if she felt she wanted to marry this man and would she be ready if he asked. She chuckled a bit and said something like, "I want to be in a committed relationship, but I don't need to get married to have that."

I took a breath and paused. "I know you don't," I said, "but he does."

"Ah ha," Andie chuckled. "Of course, he does!"

What Andie realized in that moment was that while she didn't need a formal commitment to bond to Adam (she was bonded after they began having sex), he needed to make a formal commitment to bond to her.

Andie followed my playbook and thus, set about applying the approaches and strategies needed to allow Adam to easily and naturally desire more and to think long-term. While there were times Andie just wanted to talk something out with Adam or call him up and come to a rational decision about something in their relationship, she didn't. She would reach out to me instead, and we would work out an equal strategy that did not show Andie as leading or attempting to control Adam's decisions or actions.

Though frustrating at times, Andie kept herself in check, and she communicated to Adam via actions and not words. When she did have to render her opinion, or make her needs known, she did so using the soft approached I recommended.

Women Relate Through Verbalization.
Men Relate Through Action.
#3 of Coach Paula's List of Gender Gaps

When you are independent, achieved, and self-reliant, you can easily slip into the mode of male energy, whereby you simply want to be direct and to the point. While this is effective in work and in getting a refund from a customer service rep, it can be a real turn-off to a guy with whom you're involved.

Softeners are a very effective way for you to connect to your guy. A man gets a lot of masculine energy in his daily life and doesn't look to you for more of it. Softeners allow for him to relax, relate to your femininity, and feel masculine. He has a hard time getting that anywhere else in his life, nor would you want him to. When he asks you for dinner, a response like, "No can do, sorry, I teach on Wednesday nights" is much better received when phrased a bit more softly, as in, "Oh, that would have been lovely, and that restaurant is my favorite. I'm really disappointed that I have to teach a class. I'll really miss seeing you tonight."

After a hard day at work, you might be inclined to start spewing problems over which your man has no control. It's tempting to begin venting the moment you see him: "Do you know what my stupid boss made me do today? I was working at my desk when she calls me into her office to read me the riot act about the Jetson account. She started ranting and raving and then I told her blah, blah, blah and then she said blah, blah, blah...."

This causes your guy to tune you out. He'll be much more likely to hear you, as well as commiserate and attend to your feelings about your situation if he hears, "Honey it's great to see you, but I'm so uptight from an incident at work ... would you just hold me for a few minutes while I de-stress?" This softer version allows him to do something that no one else in your life can do, and this makes him feel needed and useful. These are two things that connect him to you.

You can easily hear the difference in how these ways of relating sound. One has a harder edge, and one has a softer quality. While you can be your take-charge self at work and in many areas of life, when it comes to being with your guy, he needs you to be soft and feminine, so he can feel strong and masculine. This necessitates you becoming comfortable with feminine vulnerability.

Softeners and vulnerability take practice for many women who are used to handling everything in their lives and simply being the strong, independent women that they are. Almost daily, I find myself reminding my clients to utilize softeners and to think about the beauty of vulnerability.

As the world becomes more achievement-oriented, task-based, and less interpersonally connected, men need women to be soft and vulnerable more than ever. Think about the 80/20 rule applying to softeners. If you achieve softness around your man 80% of the time, he'll ignore the 20% of the time that you just have to be your take-charge self. The magic of a soft approach creates a lasting effect that allows your man to remain in a state of feeling achieved, confident, and useful. This can be magic to a man thinking about the possibility of a lifetime with you.

The Gift of Clients

Early on the morning of December 25th, 2016, I woke up and checked my email to find one of the best presents a dating and relationship coach can ever receive. There in my inbox was a photo of Andie's left hand with a beautiful, sparkling engagement ring that she had been given by Adam on Christmas Eve, right after her daughter had gone to bed and the two could share the moment alone.

Andie was and continues to be truly happy, and I am so happy for her. She did the work and is now reaping the rewards of her efforts. It took her one year from the time she met Adam to bring the relationship to engagement. Andie did a lot of great work, and it was a joy to help her through the inevitable highs and lows. We continue to work together because Andie knows that the work does not stop simply because she has an engagement ring, nor will it stop when she has a wedding ring.

A man's need to achieve never ends, just as a woman's need to feel desired, cherished, and honored by her man doesn't end. I continue to work with Andie as a support for the ongoing work of the day-to-day details of inspiring Adam through action and not words, and continually making him wonder and long for her in small ways. While these strategies and approaches are extremely subtle, they are crucial to the health and vitality of any long-term relationship.

The degree to which a long-term relationship will thrive is largely the degree to which a woman is willing to understand how her man loves.

I want every woman to have a relationship with commitment, desire, respect, and honor. It comes easy to a lucky few and hard-won to most. I have learned both personally and professionally that it takes women to understand the male mind so that both sexes can reap the benefits of being in a solid, loving, and committed relationship.

I believe all is possible in the world of romance because I have witnessed and experienced the amazing effects of applying the right approaches with men that allow them to love in the unique way that they do. I know because I have walked the path with my clients as they have utilized the strategies that are effective in creating commitment from the men who they love and desire.

What's Next for You?

I know that if you have read this far, you are a woman who can understand and accept the very different ways that men love and what it is that they need to experience in order to continue to feel love. Most importantly, I trust that not only do you understand and accept the vast difference in how men love and what it takes for them to commit and bond, but that you can give-over to what you need to do to create the right relationship for you and your Mr. Right – whether he is currently in your life or someone you have yet to meet!

Having come to the end of *Why Won't He Commit?,* you now have a few new tools with which to understand all aspects of how men view women, love them, commit to them, and bond. While you may have never thought you needed a new way to think about or relate to how men love, now knowing that you do might actually be a bit disappointing, if not somewhat deflating.

Even while making a living helping women effectively use the approaches and strategies that allow them to be cherished and loved by men, I struggle with the "why" of things in the world of love and romance. Why do men and women have to be so very different in their needs and wants regarding love and commitment? Why is it that women have to follow The Rules in order to be successful in having men fall for them? Why can't love be an equal sharing of pursuit by both men and women? Why is there a need for relationship coaches? Why do so many women have to suffer so much heartache and learn ways of being and interacting in order to have men commit? Why can't women just be themselves, do what they feel in the moment, and have love and commitment happen easily and naturally?

Unfortunately, there are more questions than answers. While ignorance is sometimes bliss, it can be very costly and quite heard on the heart and soul. Nature has presented us with clear preferences and behaviors. It is up to us to decide what to do with them. If we stay stuck in what seems to be the unfairness of our differences, we may never find what we are seeking. While questioning the "why" of things doesn't produce any good answers, knowing and enacting what works can turn what was once painful ignorance into current and future bliss.

Honoring What Is

I honor that you wanted to know why a man commits and why he doesn't, and that you wanted a glimpse of what it takes to further your chances of getting the divinely committed relationship that is rightfully yours! I trust that you will now begin to separate The Consumers from The Buyers in your life, and that you will be holding your head high, knowing that while a Consumer may not be ready to "adopt" you, you are a beautiful, lovable "puppy" to him and to all men.

Your time with a Buyer is on the horizon. I know that whether he is in your life now, or he is yet to be met, your Buyer is out there because you are here reading this! In other words, while a Buyer is in a state of being ready, willing, and able to commit, he will only commit to a woman who understands what she must do – and not do – to continually inspire his desire. You are becoming that woman.

You've taken the first steps towards recognizing that your way of being with a man is directly related to whether or not he will be able to experience loving you. You now know that you are beautiful and inspiring just by being the lovable "puppy" that you are, but that in order to be "the one" he will want to commit to, you will have to allow him to love in the way he loves, as a man, and not do things according to how you need to feel love, as a woman.

While you are now better prepared for the journey toward him, you are ready to understand to the depth of your soul that a man must first move towards you and be ready, willing and able to commit. You now know that your special Buyer needs to see the you that is worthy of achieving and all you need do is make him wonder about you and long for you. Sounds easy, but as with any endeavor worthy of achieving, the "devil is in the details."

Making a man wonder can be as complex as being mysterious and as elementary as not answering a text for a few hours. Making a man long for you can be as difficult as not always accepting his requests for dates despite desperately wanting to see him, or as simple as making a commitment to yourself to go to the gym, or taking a series of classes that keep you apart a few nights a week.

Now that you know what it takes for a man to feel love, what will it take for you not to be so readily available and to make a man put effort into achieving your time, attention, and affection? What are you going to do to allow a man to wonder and long for you starting tonight? Think about that for a moment. Anything worth achieving takes commitment to doing what works and not giving in to what doesn't. In other words, in order to gain commitment from a man, you must first commit to yourself – to learning, incorporating, and lovingly enacting the approaches and strategies that inspire a man's love.

Joy to the Women!

Helping women manifest commitment from the men they desire gives me great joy. My work makes me get up in the morning and feel content when I go to bed at night. A client's success is my success. For one woman, that may be reveling in her engagement that we've worked diligently to achieve, and for another, it can be simply sharing in her triumph of not texting her boyfriend when she feels anxious after a few days of not hearing from him. I celebrate each achievement like it was my own, and with each I celebrate the gift of my own good fortune of being able to do the work that I do: helping women gain committed love from men they desire.

How committed are you to manifesting commitment? Test yourself. If you haven't already, order *The Rules* and/or *Not Your Mother's Rules*. Read each and keep them and this book at the ready, to be referred to again and again. If you are in a relationship of any sort, stop doing all that you do. Simply stop. See what happens. Let me know. Email me at paula@coachpaulagrooms. com. Let's celebrate your wins – big and small. Joy to all women. Here's to you, cheers!

APPENDIX I:

Coach Paula's Cognitive Commitment Component of Men

Men Do Not Act *from* Their Feelings
or Act *on* Their Feelings.
Men Make Decisions About What
They Think Is Right for Them
and Those They Love and Care About,
Regardless of Their Feelings.

Core Principle #1

Women View Commitment as a
Natural Outgrowth of Love.
Men View Commitment as a Responsibility.

Core Principle #2

A Woman Commits Through Time
and Sex with a Man She Loves.
A Man Commits When He Has Made a Decision
that the Time Is Right for Him to Take On the
Responsibility to and for a Woman that He Loves.

Core Principle #3

In Order to Feel Good About Committing,
Women Need to Feel They Are Deeply Desired and
Are Loved, Secure, and Safe.
In Order to Feel Good About Committing,
Men Need to Feel They Have Achieved Enough
and Are Financially Prepared.
They Have Found a Woman Who They
Are Confident Will Maintain Their Interest
and Desire for the Long-Term.

Core Principle #4

A Woman Will Accept All the Attention, Caring, Time, and Sex a Man Is Willing to Give in an Attempt to Build on Her Relationship with that Man and to Determine If He Is "The One."

A Man Will Accept All the Attention, Caring, Time, and Sex a Woman Is Willing to Give for as Long as She Is Willing to Give It with No Intention Other than to Enjoy Himself (Unless He Has Decided It's the Right Time for Him to Be in a Committed Relationship).

Core Principle #5

Time, Attention, Devotion, and Great Sex Will *Increase* the Possibility of Getting a Commitment from a Woman Who Is Resistant to Being in a Committed Relationship.

Time, Attention, Devotion, and Great Sex Will *Diminish* the Possibility of Getting a Commitment from A Man Who Is Resistant to Being in a Committed Relationship.

APPENDIX II:
Coach Paula's List of Gender Gaps

1. Women love through knowing.
   Men love through wondering.

2. Women live by their feelings.
   Men live by their decisions.

3. Women relate through verbalization.
   Men relate through action.

4. Women long to cooperate, connect, and caretake.
   Men live to challenge, compete, and conquer.

5. Women bond through time and sex.
   Men bond through making a formal

commitment and then living up to their decision.

6. In order to feel deeply loved by their partner, women must feel connected, secure and cherished.
Men must feel understood, trusted and valued.

7. For women, love deepens over time.
For Men, bonding is deepened over time by continually living up to the responsibilities to which they've decided to commit.

Further Reading

All The Rules

*The Rules II: More Rules
to Live and Love By*

Not Your Mother's Rules

The Rules for Online Dating

By Ellen Fein and Sherrie Schneider:
www.therulesbook.com

Acknowledgements

Although I am grateful to many people who have given me the opportunity to write this book, there are those without whom I never would have gotten to this wonderful, albeit arduous place of putting words to paper. These special friends and family members are Brenda Fox, Bernice Grooms, Shelley Wolf, and Milad Bader and are angels that shed their grace on me throughout the process. It is only through their unending, unquestioning support that I have reached this goal.

Several years ago, Brenda Fox, along with her husband, Shane Fox, provided a haven for me to make a complete life change, without which this book would have had nary a chance of being conceived and almost certainly never achieved. Brenda's enthusiastic confidence in my message, and her personal excitement at my small achievements, was a lifeline that kept me afloat at the start of my journey.

My loving mother, Bernice Grooms, despite her own worries about a daughter going down a difficult, less-traveled path, never failed to give her support in every conceivable way. To know without a doubt that there is one person in the world who wants the world for you is a gift beyond compare. Encouraging of my reading and writing from a young age, I'm eternally grateful to have been modeled her curiosity, style, kindness, empathy, and social grace.

The beautiful soul of Shelley Wolf has guided me throughout my adult life. Without Shelley by my side lending her advice, solace, love, and messages of hope, I would certainly not be an author, a coach, a social worker, or a woman capable of helping others in the way I am fortunate enough to do. She has taught me, by example, the true meaning of friendship, caring, and non-judgmental support. If I spend the rest of my days giving whatever I can to Shelley, it will never be enough to equal what she has given to me.

Sometimes the most unique and inexplicable of friendships form that become as close as family. Milad Bader is one such friend. Milad single-handedly restored my faith in men when it was all but lost. His brotherly love, caring, and help have been there for me in ways I could not ever have imagined or hoped for in this life. I have been blessed beyond words to have met such a man and to have his support. This book is directly related to his faith in me personally, as well as professionally.

Women who have supported me in addition to those mentioned above, all with a tireless ear and open heart, who also deserve special thanks are: Elizabeth O'Neil, Martha McKittrick,

Erin Neubauer-Keys, Karen Wyeth, Lori Kupfer, and Rosie McSweeney. Along with many others, these incredible women are at the heart and soul of this work. It is only through the intuition, intelligence, and supportive guidance of the women in my life that this work has come to pass. Without the wisdom and grace of these women in particular, and of every woman who has ever shared a story of heartbreak or a triumphant success, I would not be who I am, nor doing the work I am privileged and blessed to be able to do.

Without the guidance of Angela Lauria and Maggie McReynolds, I know for certain that this book would not have made it to print. Without the exceptionally creative and indefatigable help and dedication of Micah Beals, who served as my technical advisor and all-around support, my message would not be as clear and concise as it is, and I would not be as proud as I am to have this work published.

To the Morgan James Publishing team: Special thanks to David Hancock, CEO & Founder for believing in me and my message. To my Author Relations Manager, Gayle West, thanks for making the process seamless and easy. Many more thanks to everyone else, but especially Jim Howard, Bethany Marshall, and Nickcole Watkins.

About the Author

C oach Paula Grooms, LMSW, is a Certified Personal Life Coach who specializes in Dating and Relationships. When she retired from her first career in the theater at the ripe old age of thirty, Paula became a social worker and studied solution-focused coaching.

Paula spent her teens and twenties naively believing that men and women viewed and experienced love and commitment in the same way. Following a decade of both positive and negative relationships and then an ill-fated eleven-year marriage, Paula found herself approaching forty, divorced, and starting over.

In her search to understand men and what makes for lasting relationships, Paula discovered *The Rules* by Ellen Fein and Sherrie Schneider and became a Rules Coach. The Rules provided a foundational framework from which Paula developed her unique theories and ways for women to understand how men communicate, love, and make their romantic decisions, all easily explained via relatable analogies in *Why Won't He Commit? How a Man Decides to Make You "The One."*

Paula resides in New York City and has clients in the US, Canada, Israel and Europe. She coaches via phone and skype.

Contact:

paula@coachpaulagrooms.com

www.coachpaulagrooms.com

www.facebook.com/coachpaulagrooms

www.linkedin.com/in/paula-grooms-lmsw-and-certified-personal-life-coach

www.instagram.com/coachpaulagrooms

Thank You

I hope you've gained useful information from reading *Why Won't He Commit? How a Man Decides to Make You "The One,"* and will continue your journey to find the loving and committed relationship you desire and deserve. As a reader of this book, I welcome you connecting to me with any questions you may have or comments you may wish to make.

Throughout this book, you've been reading about the two states all men live in, Consumer or Buyer. If you're looking to secure a committed relationship, it's important that you know where your man falls on the scale of being ready, willing, and able to commit. Take my Consumer vs. Buyer Relationship Test. As a thank you to readers of this book, I'm offering you this assessment and analysis for free by connecting with me at www.coachpaulagrooms.com or via www.facebook.com/coachpaulagrooms.

Morgan James
Speakers Group

www.TheMorganJamesSpeakersGroup.com

We connect Morgan James published authors with live and online events and audiences who will benefit from their expertise.

Printed in the USA
CPSIA information can be obtained
at www.ICGtesting.com
JSHW022341140824
68134JS00019B/1607